W9-DFC-567

UNFINISHED BUSINESS

Unfinished Business

NORMAN TEBBIT

WEIDENFELD AND NICOLSON
LONDON

Published in Great Britain by
George Weidenfeld & Nicolson Limited
91 Clapham High Street
London SW4 7TA

ISBN 0 297 81149 5

Printed in Great Britain by Butler & Tanner Ltd,
Frome and London

CONTENTS

INTRODUCTION

In this book I have attempted two tasks. First to make some broad assessment of the changes brought about by Thatcherism on the politics of the Conservative Party and upon the United Kingdom. Second to suggest how the reforms of 1979–1990 might usefully be continued into the 1990s.

Writing the book has underlined and clarified the essence of Thatcherism in my own mind. Looking back it can be seen not as its critics have claimed, a narrow ideological deviation from traditional Conservatism, nor as some of its supporters maintain, a 'new' Conservatism, but an inherently practical and pragmatic doctrine in the mainstream of that very broad river of Conservative thinking. Certainly Burke and Peel would have recognised in Mrs Thatcher a Conservative although they might have taken Macmillan for a Whig.

Like many Conservative doctrines in the past, Thatcherism has found its own balance between the Conservative love of individual liberty and its respect for the traditional structures and values of society. The Thatcher Conservative Party's various emphases upon aspects of each tradition have been founded on both pragmatic assessments and rebalancing to counter the socialist and neo-socialist assumptions about the nature of man and society which had become widely accepted as conventional wisdom even within the Conservative Party itself.

By the late 1970s a wide range of incentives to perverse or anti-social behaviour had been created by successive governments. Taxation had been raised to crushing levels at which, in Chancellor Healey's words, 'the pips squeaked', making tax avoidance (let alone evasion) a near necessity for individuals and businesses. Employees on modest incomes were supplied with cars and even clothes and holidays chosen less on grounds of value or utility than of tax effectiveness. Indeed, the employer himself frequently leased such chattels from companies using trading losses which had been deliberately purchased to be set against profits elsewhere. Further up the socio-economic stack, wealthy people migrated their incomes and often themselves overseas to places in which they did not wish to live to avoid taxation at levels which were all but expropriation, whilst at the bottom of the stack growing numbers of families were trapped into poverty, unemployment and the black economy by a system of tax and welfare benefits which created effective tax rates of over 100 per cent on increases in the income of low earners.

Managing individual or corporate affairs required skills somewhat like those needed to navigate one's way through a fairground crazy castle. Having laboriously clambered to success, random fiscal or regulatory trapdoors tipped businesses down into bankruptcy. In the halls of the new society the distorting mirrors of permissive norms undermined moral balance, sending upright families sprawling into disaster. Financial prudence became folly and recklessness the road to wealth as inflation robbed savers and wrote off the debts of borrowers. Victims of crime were held to be responsible for their own misfortunes by having been attractive enough to merit rape or rich enough to be robbed, whilst robber and rapist became seen as victims of society.

In short the values, structures and behavioural norms built up over centuries – based on common sense and experience – were being discarded and replaced by perverse structures and incentives which required destructive or perserve responses as a condition of survival or success.

Thatcherism was about recreating an economic and social structure in which the carrots and sticks would be applied once again to the appropriate ends of the donkey. It has been most successful where it has been most 'radical' – that is, brave enough to challenge and defeat the perverse values of the neo-socialist era with the accrued common sense of traditional norms and values.

The proposals for the future made in this book rest firmly upon the conviction that given a sane and benign social and economic structure, the behaviour of the overwhelming majority of people, institutions and corporate bodies will be socially and economically sane and benign. In offering some thoughts on the architecture of that structure, like any good Conservative I acknowledge the inherent imperfections of humanity and offer no proposals to improve the work of the deity or the impersonal forces which created us, but only ways in which society might best work within those unchangeable parameters.

CHAPTER ONE

The Conservative View

Any attempt to set out the dogma or creed of the Conservative Party risks ending in frustration and tears. More than one writer, historian, political philosopher or even practising politician has been driven to the conclusion that Conservatism is not so much a political programme as a way of looking at life or society. Even that does not resolve the difficulties since many different Conservatives through many different times have looked at society from differing viewpoints.

It fell to R. A. Butler (later Lord Butler) to re-codify Party thinking after the 1945 election defeat, and he was roundly criticised by many Conservatives for his 'pink socialism'. These days even Labour's John Smith would think it blood red rather than pink, but those were the heady days of socialism when Stalin's Russia was widely regarded as the shape of the future and Conservatism as no more than a rearguard action to delay the inevitable. In defending himself against the charge of socialism and political heresy in *The Art of The Possible* (Penguin 1973), Butler wrote:

> If my brand of Conservatism was unorthodox I was com-
> mitting heresy in remarkably good company.

That is a defence which has been rightly made by unorthodox or heretical Conservatives across the political spectrum and throughout the history of the Party. Indeed I have even made it myself.

Whilst the Conservative Party is the oldest British political party, its roots go even deeper into the past than the Party itself. Argument about how far can be endless, but many would find clearly discernible roots in the Toryism of Restoration politics. The Tories of those days held to the divine nature of the monarchy within a hierarchial and deferential society, a theme of an ordered and structured society underpinned by established institutions which has remained at the heart of Conservatism ever since. But Tory and Whig rivalry centred upon the succession controversy of the 1680s, which was decided decisively for the Whigs by the 'Glorious Revolution' of 1688. It was not until the accession of George III in 1760 that the Whig Ascendancy was broken and nearly forty years later before public alarm at the French Revolution accelerated the development of Toryism towards the beginnings of modern Conservatism.

Perhaps Bolingbroke (1678–1751), who enjoyed a chequered career as a Jacobite sympathiser and a leading opponent of the Whigs during their great Ascendancy, was amongst the first to postulate a coherent political and constitutional arrangement from a Tory point of view.

However, I would agree with those who hold Burke (1729–1797) to be the father of Conservative philosophy and Peel (1788–1850) the father of the Conservative Party. Burke, a one-time leading Whig, had broken with his Party over the extremism of Fox and the so-called New Whigs and become progressively influenced by Adam Smith, whilst Peel having fought and won the battle against protectionism and set a framework for modern Conservatism was then rejected by his Party.

I have also always had some affection for John Reeves (1752–1829). Somewhat of an opportunist, like others of his time he combined what would be seen today as several imcompatible careers as an historian, civil servant, quango-member, member of the judiciary and political commentator. His letters on *The English Government* have about them some timeless truths, none better than on the fate of left-wing would-be radical reformers when saddled with office:

> For when the Whigs came into office they found nothing of the Constitution and the Revolution principles with which they had been used to amuse themselves ... For it is a sad truth to be told to those gentlemen who are running the career of Opposition with great eminence of talent and display of ability ... when they are in office they must have done with mere words and must come to things; they must set down to work by line and rule; must search Laws; hunt precedents, examine minutes of proceedings, consult and discuss and pursue a detail; often submitting themselves to the advice of subordinated persons. ...

To me that has about it the ring not of Disraeli's cry for Tory men and Liberal measures but Liberal men and Tory measures.

Burke well understood the limitations on the power of governments to achieve good, and the likelihood of their causing harm whilst seeking good. Who could not warm to his passionate denunciation of the poverty lobby of his own day?

> Nothing can be so base and so wicked as the political canting language, the Labouring Poor. Let compassion be shewn in action, the more the better, according to every man's ability, but let there be no lamentation of their

condition. It is no relief to their miserable circumstances; it is only an insult to their miserable understandings. It arises from a total want of charity, or a total want of thought. Want of one kind was never relieved by want of any other kind. Patience, labour, sobriety, frugality and religion should be recommended to them; all the rest is downright fraud.

As he observed (and Beveridge found a century and a half later), if 'the state supported the people, once used to that support people might never be satisfied to have it otherwise'.

The influence of Adam Smith can be seen clearly in Burke's belief in the immutable laws of supply and demand, which with wisdom still lacking amongst most trades union leaders and contemporary Labour politicians he clearly saw must apply to wages – the price of labour being a commodity like any other. Burke, like Thatcher (and perhaps Callaghan in the end) but not Macmillan, Heath nor Kinnock, realised that whilst it was possible to persuade Parliament to repeal the law of supply and demand it could not prevent it from having effect. Indeed, as Burke argued, to interfere with its operation is to invite an inevitable backlash.

Naturally enough in the context of his times Burke saw private charity as a Christian obligation upon those better off, clearly feeling that charity, like mercy, is twice blessed. Whilst there is undoubtedly a place still for charity in the relief of need, there can be few who could believe that in the secular society of today it could adequately replace the Department of Social Security. What is less widely recognised (or at least not publicly admitted) is that there is a considerable price to pay, and not just in economic terms, for state intervention to treat the symptoms of poverty through welfare.

Burke's approach to the basic, fundamental and everlasting laws of economics and much more besides, is as valid and central to Conservatism today as it was two hundred years ago. The question which he regarded as the most important which legislators should ask themselves, remains at the centre of the political debate today:

> What the State ought to take upon itself to direct by the public wisdom and what it ought to leave with as little interference as possible to individual discretion.

His own answer to that question still has considerable appeal:

> ... the clearest line of distribution which I could draw ... was this: That the State ought to confine itself to what regards the State, or the creatures of the State, namely, the exterior establishment of its religion; its magistracy; its revenue; its military force by sea and land and corporations that owe their existence to its fiat; in a word, to everything that is truly and properly public, to the public peace, to the public safety, to the public order, to the public prosperity....

What is remarkable about so much of what Burke wrote and said is not that in some particulars here and there it might need updating to the late twentieth century, but that its drive and thrust have been the drive and thrust of the most successful period of Conservatism for a hundred years, the Thatcher administration of 1979–1990.

In the years after the death of Burke, Lord Liverpool's early nineteenth-century administrations were not rich in the excitement of political philosophical debate, but his resignation in 1827 left something of a power vacuum which Peel determined to fill. In doing so he emerged as the foremost of the Tory – or Conservative Party (as it soon became known) – leaders of the first half of the century. Most Tories of the day deeply mistrusted and opposed the great changes of the Reform Act of 1832. The Tory paternalists sought then, as in later times, to create a coalition of the wealthy landowning aristocracy and the poor working classes. The workers were to be saved from both the dangers of democracy and of exploitation by the capitalist middle classes and hopefully the aristocracy and its wealth would be saved from the vulgar capitalist nouveau riche and revolution alike. The creation of wealth was given little encouragement; after all, the aristocracy had plenty and the workers would be corrupted, getting above themselves if they had too much. The 1832 reforms were feared for the power which they might give to the middle and the better-off working classes and take from the wealthy landowners by the abolition of rotten boroughs and with it the right to buy seats in Parliament.

Peel shared the concern that the reforms might destabilise society but once the Act was passed it was not long before Tory pragmatism asserted itself, accepting the reforms and looking to take advantage of them. However, Peel's economic views soon brought him into sharp dispute with the Tory paternalists. For him the problems of poverty could be dealt with only within a market system. He no more believed in the benevolence of the baker or butcher than did Adam Smith.

When William IV invited him to form a new administration to replace the Whigs Peel sought to create an alliance positioned in the centre of the social structure rather than composed of its outer wings. Ahead of his times as usual, Peel issued in rather modern style an election manifesto to his constituents at Tamworth and the wider world. The Tamworth Manifesto is not a particularly exciting document and although its name is often incanted by the left of the modern Conservative Party it does not set out a paternalist or interventionist case.

Peel's first administration was short-lived and it was after his defeat that he began to articulate more clearly his views which grew naturally from those of Burke. Indeed it may be that Peel's social and political views, like those of Burke, were shaped by his economic beliefs, which rested in turn upon the work of Adam Smith.

There can be no doubt about his attachment to market economics – most notably the law of supply and demand, and it was that which made inevitable his dispute with the old Tory paternalists. The nature of that dispute is admirably described by Robert Eccleshall, Reader and Head of the Department of Politics at Queen's University, Belfast:

> But whereas writers such as Burke and Reeves had extolled the social and political functions of 'chieftains' as a means of rallying the propertied classes against the threat of radical populism, Tory paternalists now accused one section of the governing elite of abdicating its responsibilities for the common people. The social fabric was threatened less by the potentially unruly masses, they supposed, than by the devotees of political economy intent on displacing the affective ties associated with landed proprietorship by the harsh impersonal relations of the capitalist market. Hence their desire for a concordat between rich and poor in opposition to the industrial middle classes and their allies, including the Peelite wing of the Conservative Party.[1]

Indeed, with the substitution of 'Thatcherite' for 'Peelite' it is not a bad description of the Wet versus Dry struggle of the 1980s.

Peel stood ever more firmly in favour of the disciplined society and the free market, concepts not incompatible, but often jostling with each other then as now. But it was the controversy over agricultural tariffs, epitomised by the Corn Laws dispute, which took him steadily towards what we would call today the Thatcherite view. The tariff on corn had been

[1] *English Conservatism Since the Restoration* (Unwin Hyman, 1990).

halved in 1842 but the distress of the Irish potato famine forced Peel's hand to go further. The issue split the Tory Party and Corn Law repeal was achieved only with the support of the new Liberals.

That was the last straw for the Tory 'Ultras' (the Wets of their day). An exclusive, snobbish, paternalistic faction, they had barely tolerated Peel since as Liverpool's Home Secretary he had first repealed the anti-Catholic Test and Corporation Act and then legislated to allow Catholics to sit in the Commons. Such was their distress that the Ultras even contemplated an anti-Tory alliance with the Whigs.

In the end after Peel's death, his Peelite Tories joined the newly established Liberals who in turn became the custodians of a good deal of the wisdom of Adam Smith and Burke for much of the nineteenth century.

The Tories, or Conservatives as they now styled themselves, fell increasingly under the influence of the romantic paternalists. Lord John Manners, Sadler and to some extent Shaftesbury (Lord Ashley as he then was) became the driving force of a Conservative philosophy in some ways forward-looking and in others harking back to a mythical Merrie England, in which the aristocracy were kindly and benevolent landowners, prepared to shoulder the onerous responsibility of wealth and power, and the workers were simple but decent peasants lacking the ambition or ability to change their lot, and grateful to their betters for guidance and protection against indecent ambition and greedy capitalism.

One can wonder to what extent, conviction, convenience, coincidence and ambition brought Disraeli (1804–1881) in to the anti-Peelite faction. The romantic style of his novels certainly matched the mood of many Conservatives uneasy at the radical changes of the late eighteenth and early nineteenth centuries. The upset of the natural order of things precipitated by the industrial revolution, the growth of the great cities, the new wealthy industrialists, and both the prosperous urban workers and the urban poor, fermented a great insecurity and a longing for the old certainties of former times.

Disraeli's genius was in his ability to ride two horses at once, switching from the romanticism of a rosy tinted vision of a Merrie England which never was, to the Empire, the Queen Empress Victoria and Britain's imperial destiny.

In his early days Disraeli's politics had twisted and turned and at one time he was a staunch supporter of both the landed interest and the Corn Laws, but later he turned against protectionism, and then not least by his 1867 Reform Act and numerous legislative acts of social reform, secured a following amongst the better-off working classes.

At one time or another Disraeli was most things to most men. Certainly he was a reformer, but perhaps above all an outsider desperate to be an insider and an opportunist. None the less, he steered the Conservative Party back to the centre stage of politics, persuading it of the need to stay ahead of the game by outpacing the Liberals on social reform and seeking political support amongst the newly enfranchised classes. Few leaders played the patriotic card more skilfully, using the Empire and Monarchy to generate a colourful pride of belonging which contrasted so well with what often appeared to be a monochrome Liberal image. Once he had gone, however, the Conservative Party was again left lacking in direction.

The Liberals had fallen upon hard times in 1886 when the Party split over Home Rule, bringing about the alliance of Conservatives and Liberal Unionists. Not only did that lead to twenty years of Conservative dominance, but for a while the Party's direction was supplied by Liberal Unionist Joseph Chamberlain (1836–1914). He was a paternalist who took the Party back from free trade to the protectionism of the early nineteenth century with his campaign for tariff reform and Imperial Preference. Perhaps that for the first time gave the

Conservatives an appeal to the manufacturing interest. However, the free traders fought back and a divided Party lost the key 1906 election which saw the emergence of Labour as a significant force.

For most of the early twentieth century the Conservative Party was in turmoil, with free traders and protectionists, paternalists and *laissez faire* Conservatives or industrialists (what we might today call Selsdonites or Thatcherites) unable to agree and too evenly balanced for a clear direction of policy to be achieved.

Having fought and lost the 1910 election on a programme of tariff reform the Party then wobbled away from protectionism. The Home Rule controversy also continued to exercise its malign influence and, not least due to Carson, the Party looked confused and uncertain. Not surprisingly all manner of groups sprang up peddling their own variants of policy with none having the muscle to achieve a clear ascendancy. Searching through the works and words of Balfour, F. E. Smith, Randolph Churchill, let alone many less well known but influential writers of the period, it is hard to find the common threads of Conservatism. Somewhere within all of them there is a theme of respect for the established institutions of the State and a concern for the maintenance of order and protection of property in what were times of tumultuous change, but not too much else in common. Either everyone was in Butler's terms a heretic, or heresy was itself an orthodoxy.

Setting out the individualist argument Balfour (1848–1930) pledged himself to

> resist the usurpation of power by government, or the subjection either of the individual or the minority, to coercion on the part of the majority. . . .

and to the belief that

the only safe path of progress lies in the continued advance of that freedom and in the ever increasing emancipation of the individual from interference by the community in the management of his personal affairs. ...

And in his condemnation of the levelling policies of socialism as the road to pauperisation, we can hear a pre-echo of Mrs Thatcher's condemnation of the pocket-money society:

Will men work for the collective benefit who will not work for their own? ... Does it not stand to reason that if men who strive are to get no more personal advantage than those who do not, it would not only appear but would be, absurd to strive at all.

Personal advantage is really the sole motive power to the immense majority, and so it will remain.

In contrast F. E. Smith (later Lord Birkenhead) spoke for the paternalists, again using almost the words later to be used by Macmillan:

We have to deal with men, not with ideas; with the urgent necessities of today, not with the theories of the past or bubble hopes of the future. In all things we stand midway between conflicting extremes. We are not for the classes or the masses, for their interests are one. We are not for Individualism or Socialism for neither is founded on fact. We stand for the State and for the unity which, whether in the form of kingdom or empire or class solidarity, the State alone can bring. Above all stands the State and in that lies the essence of Toryism. Our ancestors left it to us, and not the least potent method of preserving it is to link the conception of State Toryism with the practice of Social Reform.

As the appalling carnage of the First World War ended and the brief inter-war years began, the Conservative Party was no nearer to finding its new philosophical beliefs. However, when the wartime coalition with the Liberals was ended in 1922 it began another period of Conservative election success and the extinction of the Liberals as a governing party. Apart from the Labour minority governments of 1923–4 and 1929–31, the Conservatives held office either in their own right or as the leading coalition partner until the last months of the Second World War in 1945.

After Bonar Law's ill health brought about his resignation as the first post-war leader and Prime Minister in 1923, the Conservative leadership fell first to Baldwin (1867–1947) and then in 1937 to Neville Chamberlain (the son of Joseph).

The debate over policy was overwhelmingly influenced by the aftermath of the war, the slump and the rise of Hitler and National Socialism in Germany. Baldwin's style was essentially conciliatory common sense and undogmatic. Neville Chamberlain (1869–1940), like his father Joseph, was protectionist and paternalist but the libertarian free trade cause lacked front-ranking national champions. Ernest Benn, uncle of the former Viscount Stansgate, left-wing socialist, Tony (Anthony Wedgewood) Benn, was a spirited advocate of the doctrines of Spencer who had founded the Liberty and Property Defence League in the late 1880s. Ernest Benn summed up the prevailing view of the day in two sentences, 'Does the man keep the state or can the state keep the man? All Victorian parties accepted the first solution and rejected the second absolutely; all twentieth century parties have denied or doubted the first and all, in varying degrees, have accepted the second.' However the political running continued to be made by the new extreme paternalists, most notably Harold Macmillan (1894–1956), later Earl Stockton.

There is little doubt that Macmillan was deeply affected by his experience on the battlefields of the First World War and by the suffering brought about by the depression of the inter-war years. Both seem to have confirmed him in his paternalism and in his views of class superiority. No one could doubt his affection for the men placed under his command in the Army, nor that he saw himself and his class as the natural superiors and leaders of the common soldiers. His conviction that birth mattered more than brains remained with him throughout his life and his politics, like those of the Whigs, were as much about the protection of the privileges of his own class, as the protection of the lower classes against exploitation by entre-preneurial capitalists of the kind who had created the wealth which he had inherited.

Macmillan's policy was that of 'the middle way', a corporatist route somewhere between Marxism and *laissez faire* capitalism. Corporatism was fashionable between the wars being not only at the roots of the economic policies of Franco, Mussolini and Hitler, but widely supported in Britain too. Not only was there sympathy for Hitler in some right-wing circles but it was the former Labour Party Minister Oswald Mosley who founded the British Fascist movement. Macmillan (a corporatist in my view) was an early advocate of national councils for industry of the kind established within the National Economic Develop-ment Council after the Second World War, although his indus-trial councils would have had powers to control prices and output. However, it is in *The Middle Way* that he sets out corporatist ideals and views most clearly. Whilst he argued for 'the deliberate preservation of private enterprise in a field lying outside the range of minimum human needs' (presumably for food, water, housing, clothing, electricity, gas and transport), he declined to defend the virtues of private enterprise in the fields for which it is suited, even

> to condone or excuse the poverty and insecurity in the basic necessities of life which we have today as a legacy

of unrestrained competition and uneconomic waste and redundancy. I shall advocate all the more passionately on grounds of morality, of social responsibility as well as of economic wisdom, a wide extension of social enterprise and control in the sphere of minimum human needs. The satisfaction of those needs is a duty which society owes to its citizens. In carrying out that responsibility it should adopt the most economical methods of large scale co-operative enterprise. The volume of the supply of these necessities, the prices at which they are sold, and the power of the consumer to buy them should not be left to the determination of competitive effort. We have to evolve a new system by which the supply of those articles which we have classified as being of common need and more or less standardised in character, would be absorbed into an amplified conception of social services. . . .

Britain has been moving along the road towards economic planning for many years now ... Unless we can continue this peaceful evolution from a free capitalism to a planned capitalism, or, it may be, a new synthesis of Capitalist and Socialist theory, there will be little hope of preserving the civil democratic and cultural freedom which limited as it may be at the moment by economic inefficiency is a valuable heritage.

So much for Burke and Peel.

Many others fell under the same influences. Julian Amery (1919–) as a young student at Oxford issued with others a 'Statement of The Principles of a New Conservatism' which was approved by the University Conservative Association:

We reaffirm the mediaeval distinction between the ownership and use of Capital, believing that the State has the right to control any part of the economic life of its citizens. In principle we neither support nor oppose nationalisation of industry, but where it is a means of raising the standard of living, we shall not hesitate to employ it.

The statement also called for the 'subsidising of organised export drives and of shipping and the extension of the rationalising principle through nationally controlled marketing boards'.

Quintin Hogg (latterly Lord Hailsham) tells in his memoirs *A Sparrow's Flight* that he too 'was for a long time a determined supporter of Macmillan's Middle Way' but that he realised it was a fallacious analysis and that the Conservative Party should 'roll back the frontiers of the State during periods of Conservative rule by reversing the ratchet effect', although this meant 'turning the Conservative Party from its traditional conservatism into a party of change committed to ... turning back the whole bias of society to something nearer the ideal of the Liberals of the previous century'.

The Second World War strengthened the hand of the paternalists and neo-socialists seeking the compromise between Marxism and Capitalism. It was a period in which the intellectual establishment had broadly accepted that capitalism had had its day and that Marxism was indeed the way of the future.

The Conservative defeat of 1945 did little to alter that prevailing view. Although there was a considerable degree of deregulation and repeal of wartime controls during the first post-war Conservative Government of 1951–55, the complacent corporatist stance of Macmillan smothered all attempts to steer away from the near consensus which arose between the Labour Party of Gaitskell and the political thinking of R. A. Butler (1902–82). Indeed the word 'Butskellism' was coined to describe the policies of both parties.

Yet somewhere, something was stirring within the Conservative Party. Here and there Conservatives were reading Hayek whose masterful work *The Road to Serfdom*, written during the war years, was so far ahead of its time. Amongst the first politicians to argue the liberal individualist case was Enoch Powell (1912–). However, it was not until 1970 under Mr Heath's leadership that the Party presented an election programme, the Selsdon Manifesto, which marked a clear break from the past. Unhappily Mr Heath abandoned that programme, returning to corporatism and suffering defeat within four years.

By then the political climate was changing. Keith Joseph (1918–) (later Lord Joseph) later observed that he had thought he was a Conservative but he had not really been one until his 'conversion' in 1974. With the election of Mrs Thatcher as Conservative leader in 1975 and Prime Minister in 1979 the liberal wing gained the ascendency, but not even at the height of her power were the paternalists and corporatists – or wets as they had become known – totally defeated.

Thatcherism was not some new and atypical development within the Conservative Party. It was a return to the thinking of Burke and Peel, to the policies of the liberal free traders and a rejection of the politics of the modern whigs and 'middle-wayers'.

It is essentially Conservative in its respect for the established institutions and the constitutional settlement and its support for an ordered, law-abiding society, albeit one structured to encourage social mobility. It is Conservatism too in its patriotism, a patriotism shared with most Labour voters, but an embarrassment amongst many of Labour's activists.

Perhaps what marked Thatcherism most clearly was not its beliefs, but its willingness to fight for them. If we opposed nationalisation (which we did) and if it has proved a costly failure (and it has) then it should be reversed. Similarly if inflation is not merely an economic enemy but a social enemy too, then it should be stopped. And if the powers of trades unions are excessive then trim them back.

What has been remarkable is the intellectual dominance gained from such single-minded pursuit of principles. John Boyd-Carpenter once called for a middle way between Manchester and Moscow. In political terms Mrs Thatcher moved Moscow and with it the location of that holy grail of the paternalist and corporatist, the white line down the middle of the political road.

In doing so Mrs Thatcher and her adherents trod on many toes. Too many of the new Conservatives were political outsiders and many of them cared little for the offence which they gave to the old failed establishment.

The economic policies of the 1980s created a great deal of new wealth which challenged the supremacy of old wealth – a source of discontent amongst old wealth and the poor alike.

In the second chapter of this book I have sought to set out what the Thatcherites achieved.

CHAPTER TWO

The Thatcher Years at Home

Arguments over the extent and the desirability of the changes brought about during Margaret Thatcher's administration will continue for many years. Many of her critics are torn between either claiming she changed nothing or attributing to her the destruction of local government, the National Health Service, the State school system, the trades union movement, manufacturing industry, public sector housing, indeed life as we know it. Many of her admirers whilst claiming she changed the world in a way which no other politician could have done, show very little confidence that the spirit of her days and the changes she wrought will for long outlast her days in office.

The truth is more complicated and still difficult to assess. As usual the statistics, the mere description of events by numbers, can be arranged to tell more stories than one. In this case the truth is not just an objective matter but a subjective one too, a matter of moods and feelings, values, assumptions and qualities as much as a matter of quantities and numbers, important as they are.

To encapsulate the Thatcher years, to savour their essence, needs hardly more than a sentence.

When she entered Downing Street in 1979, Liverpool was not remarkable, but typical of Britain, but when she left, only Liverpool remained still locked in the world of the 1970s.

Liverpool's trades union leaders of 1991 crowing atop piles of stinking uncollected rubbish like cockerels on dung heaps, its welfare mentality growing upon the destruction of wealth producing jobs, the growth of dependence upon the 'Corpy' (the Corporation of Liverpool), poverty and crime nourished on the thin gruel of welfare, the whole mess financed by borrowing whose costs choke any tentative growth of industry or commerce, all that which today we see as a sickness isolated on Merseyside, was the world's image and the terrible reality of Britain in the late 1970s. And the Labour Militants, from whom Mr Kinnock and the modern Labour Party affect to draw away their coats for fear of contamination, were the Labour orthodoxy which, in the 1970s, Mr Kinnock and his friends warmly embraced and nurtured, and which in turn led him to the Party leadership.

There is not, nor ever has been, any folly committed in Liverpool in the 1980s which was not applauded by the Labour Party in the late 70s and very few which were not practised by the last Labour Government in Westminster in the early 70s. Nor is there any policy espoused over the years by its Militant administration which was not formerly upheld by most, if not all, of Labour's shadow cabinet of today.

That London – and Britain – is not like Liverpool today and that the Labour Party dare no longer own up to its socialist soul is the most graphic and dramatic encapsulation of what was achieved in Margaret Thatcher's time.

With unconscious irony Mr Kinnock himself most vividly portrayed the change and how it had been achieved. Defending the decision of the 'moderate' Labour council to contract out

Liverpool's refuse collection service to private enterprise in clear breach of his own national policy of no privatisation, Mr Kinnock explained that the predicament of debt laden, strike bound, run down Liverpool was so dire that privatisation was the only path. Elsewhere he pointed out, things are nowhere so bad (and especially not in the NHS) that private enterprise needs to be brought in to rescue the people from disaster.

In 1991 the political debate has been about when the recession would end but in 1979 it was over whether Britain was governable. Harold Wilson in 1969 had attempted to bring back under the law the trades union barons whose metaphorical tanks were forever on the lawn of No. 10 Downing Street, but was turned over in Cabinet by their special representatives. He lost power a year later. Mr Heath successfully legislated to the same end but his laws were upended by the striking miners and when he asked the electors 'who governs?' they thought it safest to answer 'not you' and he was bundled out of office. Within six years Mr Callaghan, his rhetoric sharpened by his monetarist son-in-law, Peter Jay, and his resolve stiffened by the bailiffs of the International Monetary Fund whose help he had been compelled to seek, fought the same unruly union barons for his survival through the winter of discontent – and lost.

No-one these days asks if Britain is governable. Indeed the frequent complaint of the Opposition was that Mrs Thatcher as the elected Prime Minister, had a habit of having her own way and exhibited a reluctance to let Parliament be overruled by extra parliamentary forces.

A factor in the success of the Thatcher years was the closer coupling of cause and effect in the minds of the voters. High government spending was linked to high taxation and high government borrowing – and therefore to high inflation. High spending councils were linked to high rates, although the making of the even tighter linkage between higher council spending and high community charges was badly bungled, and became an important factor in the overthrow of Margaret Thatcher.

Low productivity was linked to low wages and bad industrial relations which lost customers and thereby lost jobs. Risk taking, skill, entrepreneurship and hard work were linked to high rewards.

It was not all success. The public relations battles over the Health Service and education were fought too often and for too long over claims of how much was being spent rather than what was achieved. The workings of the market created by benefit payments (dealt with in Chapter 6) was never explained or even acknowledged, and the role of subsidies in raising costs (and eventually prices) was not openly explained.

The bare statistics of 1979–1990 contain many illustrations and some measurements of the Thatcher changes. Many can be either discounted or given premium value, since economic statistics depend crucially upon the stage of the economic cycle at the times of comparison and the influence of the inheritance of one government from another.

None the less some things are quite clear. Public debt repayment was not a feature of post-war British governments before 1979. Indeed in Labour's last year of office the Government borrowed £9.2 billion which in today's money would be approaching £30 billion. Although in the current recession (as Keynes would have advised) there will be substantial budget deficits, during the boom years (again with Keynesian approval) substantial debt repayments amounting to some £25 billion were made. Already national debt as a proportion of GDP is lower than at any time since the First World War, and the standards by which budget policy is now judged have been shifted significantly. Debt repayment in boom years is accepted as normal and a PSBR of £30 billion would be regarded as absurd.

The reduction of the share of GDP taken by government

expenditure did not prove easy. In 1975–6 it had peaked at over 49 per cent (more than 11 percentage points up over ten years) but under IMF instructions it had eased down to 44 per cent by Labour's last year, 1978–9. The savings made during the Thatcher years – most notably on subsidies to nationalised industries – have been largely eaten up by the increased costs of welfare, the NHS and recession. By 1982–3 the share peaked at $47\frac{1}{2}$ per cent falling back to $38\frac{1}{2}$ per cent in 1989–90 (the lowest level for twenty-three years) then rising again under the impact of recession to a forecast of $41\frac{1}{2}$ per cent for 1991–2. There is no doubt however of the determination of the Government to return to the path of the reduction of the share of GDP spent by the State, nor that governments of any party would now be judged by the standards set during the Thatcher years.

Success in that area and a greater burden placed on indirect taxes has made possible the cutting of the standard rate of income tax from 33 per cent to 25 per cent and the institution of a single higher rate of 40 per cent in contrast to the former nine rate structure which rose to 83 per cent with a further 16 per cent surcharge on investment income making a top rate of 98 per cent. From income tax rates amongst the highest in the world Britain has now been delivered into rates amongst the lowest in the world.

By 1979 Britain had not only the highest tax rates in the democratic non-communist world but the largest public sector of industry. Over the years after 1945 the state sector of industry had grown in size encompassing not just the old heavy industries but shipbuilding, ports, air, road and rail transport, motor cars and aerospace, with forays through the National Enterprise Board into electronics, publishing, office equipment and more besides. The conventional wisdom was that nationalisation could not be reversed. The nationalisation, denationalisation and renationalisation of steel, it was said, had established that and the public disapproved of 'ping pong politics'. The business of Conservative governments was seen to be to improve the management of nationalised industries, not to liberate them from the state back into ownership by the public. Mr Heath bravely set out in 1970 committed to a policy of denationalisation but having liberated the Carlisle Breweries and Thomas Cook Limited his courage failed him and his government nationalised Rolls Royce.

The Labour Government which followed Mr Heath continued the process of nationalisation taking over aerospace, construction and shipbuilding. Its narrow majority prevented the other nationalisation measures proposed in 1974, including the whole or part of the building and construction, machine tool, pharmaceutical, road haulage and North Sea oil and gas industries as well as at least one bank and building society.

Since 1979 the process has been triumphantly reversed.

British Airways, British Telecom, British Gas, British Steel, British Aerospace, British Airports Authority, Rolls Royce, Harland and Wolff, Cable and Wireless, The National Freight Company, The Rover Group (formerly British Leyland), Amersham International, Enterprise Oil, the water supply industry and both the electricity generation and distribution industries as well as the nationalised ports and numerous businesses in road passenger transport, shipbuilding, ship repair and smaller firms in other industries have been sold. The portfolio of the National Enterprise Board has been disposed of and the Board itself has gone. Almost without exception the performance of the denationalised firms has improved. Only in a tiny number of cases (almost all in the extremely depressed shipbuilding and repair industry) have the privatised companies fallen into serious difficulties.

When the programme began it was not only condemned as mistaken but derided as impossible. Indeed few Conservatives believed it could be achieved on such a scale and to such an extent. The foolish blatherings about 'selling the family silver' are no longer heard as the former nationalised industries which sucked money out of the taxpayer (British Steel alone was at one time subsidised at a rate of over £1.5 billion a year) now contribute their share of tax to finance expenditure on health, education, defence and welfare etc. In the case of British Telecom alone that contribution in the year 1990–1 amounted to just under £1 billion in tax and some £400 million in dividends on the remaining government shareholding. In addition the £4 billion which was the proceeds of the original flotation has been saving the taxpayer almost half a billion a year in interest charges which would have been due had the Government kept the family silver locked up in the vaults and borrowed to finance expenditure instead.

Reference is made elsewhere to the importance of the trades union reform legislation of the 1980s. It played a crucial role in the defeat of the coal strike which itself was a historic event in British post war history. The 1984 Act, based on my earlier White Paper, was not fully in effect as the strike began, which allowed Scargill to ferment a national strike without direct risk to union funds without a national ballot. However the combination of the 1982 and 1984 Acts largely prevented secondary and sympathetic action by railwaymen, and brought about the defeat of all attempts to call a national dock strike. In addition the inspired leadership by Bob Haslem and Bob Scholey* of British Steel and the courageous conduct of steel workers and their union leaders, assisted by the new laws, kept the steel industry going through appalling difficulties.

Until then it had been an axiom of British politics that the miners would always win a strike and had to be bought off. Since then it has been different, and although good planning by Nigel Lawson, Peter Walker, Ian MacGregor played its part

* Later Lord Haslem and Sir Robert Scholey.

the credit falls overwhelmingly to Margaret Thatcher. No other leader would have backed the legal changes which prevented the secondary action which would have made a coal strike effective and I think none other would have had the courage to fight the dispute through to victory.

All these changes, and as Nicholas Ridley has argued in his book *My Style of Government*, a floating exchange rate, brought about the remarkable decade of economic growth and rising living standards.

Although the growth years, unmatched in Britain's postwar history, boiled over into the inflationary problem and the recession of 1990, real economic progress was made. Living standards increased sharply, the average family man with a wife and two children enjoyed an increase of more than a third in real net take home pay. Agreeable as that outcome appears there are even more encouraging trends behind it. First, for the first time since the end of the Second World War we have achieved a sustained period of higher economic growth than our leading European competitors and, second, even after the boil over into inflation, the Thatcher record on that measurement was markedly better than that of her Labour predecessors from 1974 to 1979. In fact the average of Thatcher inflation was only half of Labour's figure.

Productivity gains also matched and often exceeded those of our competitors and once the industrial relations reforms began to bite and the coal strike of 1984–5 collapsed, Britain's record as a strike happy country where unions ran riot became only a memory. Before the Thatcher era bad industrial relations had become the biggest single barrier to inward investment and a major factor in persuading British business to invest overseas rather than at home. Since the mid-Eighties our good industrial relations have become a prime factor in attracting overseas investment.

Amongst other 'business friendly' changes, the simplification and stabilisation of corporate taxation reflected in the low rate (35 per cent) and non-discriminatory nature of corporation tax and the reduction of regulatory burdens have not merely marked a clear change of direction from earlier years but have helped to give Britain the most favourable business climate in Europe. It is too easily forgotten that when Margaret Thatcher came into office the Government had powers over pay, prices and dividends, and controls over the movement of capital, all of which were abolished alongside most of those over bank lending and hire purchase.

These changes promoted the expansion of self employment and the creation of new enterprises. For many years small businesses and self employment had languished or declined, the regulatory and taxation system, union hostility and high inflation proving too much for most would-be entrepreneurs to establish themselves. Indeed it was commonly believed that the British no longer saw themselves as business people running their own firms, but only as employees. However hard working and ambitious to get to the top they might be, it was the top of someone else's business or some branch of government. Today despite the recent recession, the number of new small businesses is still increasing and self-employment is now some three and a quarter million against less than two million in 1979.

Alongside the changing attitude to being one's own boss has been a change towards the idea of share ownership. Although a great deal more remains to be done a vital threshold has been crossed with many millions of people who had never thought of themselves as shareholders having acquired shares in one or more of the privatisations or flotations such as that of Abbey National. The precise number of shareholders is not easy to ascertain, but it is certainly over ten million – more than treble the 1979 total. Too few of the new shareholders have anything approaching a portfolio and most of the holdings are very small, but an idea has been planted and is taking root. Employee share schemes have multiplied almost two hundred fold to approaching 6,000 and together with personal equity plans have done much to build on the success of the privatisation issues.

The wider spread of ownership of wealth has also been promoted by personal pension schemes (over 3.5 million) and perhaps above all by increasing home ownership, now over 65 per cent, assisted by the sale of almost one and a half million public sector houses.

Few people seem yet to have fully appreciated the extent of the social and economic changes implicit in these bare statistics.

My own generation of working-class people had no expectation of inheriting any worthwhile wealth from our parents. That older generation lived mostly in rented accommodation. The more fortunate enjoyed a very modest occupational pension, might have saved a modest sum deposited at the bank, building society or in national savings, and might have enough in an insurance policy 'to provide for a decent funeral'. All too many had little more at the end of their lives than at the beginning and certainly did not leave enough to affect the lives of their children. The generation now entering their retirement years, let alone those to come, will increasingly leave to their children houses and even shares as well as those traditional small savings. Their children, already owner occupiers, will thus inherit quite useful sums of money – even modest former council houses in the London suburbs are worth more than £50,000, perhaps as much as £100,000 – which, even divided between the average family, can become the source of renewed savings and investment or enhanced spending power. In short Thatcher's working-class children will be the first of their kind to inherit wealth from their parents.

That generation, now in their thirties, have a standard of life almost unthinkable to their parents at that age in the early '60s, let alone their grandparents in the 1930s. Enjoying home ownership, a growing stock of capital, and purchasing power

31

giving access to mobility through car ownership, the convenience of telephones, dishwashers, clothes washers and driers (the Monday morning clothes line seems to have gone the way of clogs and gas lights), holidays in the sunshine and much more besides.

They are accustomed to the ideas of self-employment and ownership of – or employment within small businesses. Trades union membership is no longer regarded as a cultural necessity and the number of union members has fallen from over 13 million to only 10 million. At most, membership is now seen as a convenience – an insurance against gross unfairness by an employer and a system of wage bargaining in larger businesses, but no longer are union leaders seen as political leaders. Indeed, the designation of 'leader' is perhaps no longer quite appropriate. The union members seem to have used the powers given them by my legislation to reassert themselves as owners of the union, regarding the leadership as servants not masters of the members. As in all democratic systems, things do not always go perfectly but there are now self-correcting mechanisms. The new legal provisions breaking the power of the closed shop, giving members the right to elect directly the leadership and giving, in effect though not in so many words, a right to ballot before strike action, have changed the balance of power within unions.

Strike action is now seen as a weapon of the last, not the first, resort. Co-operation with management, not confrontation, has become a preferred choice to improve pay and conditions. Indeed to be on strike is now regarded as a miscalculation if not a misfortune, where once it was not just the norm but a badge of 'working class solidarity', perhaps even manhood.

There have been three other changes of perception or attitude which have been insufficiently appreciated.

First, the idea of nationalisation as a way of improving services to consumers or the prospects of employees is all but stone dead. Privatisation may have been smeared by the attacks of Labour, Tory paternalists and some free market Tories concerned at the regulation of neo-monopolies, but it is now regarded as the natural way to improve services and cut costs. For the first time in its history Labour no longer dares openly to propose nationalisation, even though it cannot bring itself to renounce it.

Second, inflation is now regarded not only as the 'enemy' of economic success, but it is seen as an evil which can be overcome. Indeed at an NEDC meeting in June 1991 unions and employers combined to push on to the Chancellor a commitment to hold inflation between zero and 3 per cent. Such an agreed aim would have been impossible in the late '70s. In those days inflation had become taken for granted as the normal and inevitable, and single figure increases in the Retail Price Index were claimed as triumphant success. The accountancy profession, egged on by government, produced a new system of current cost accountancy, designed to help business live with the destabilising effects of double digit inflation. It has now been totally discarded.

Third, in contrast to the days when Prime Minister Heath panicked at the prospect of one million registered as unemployed, figures of two and three million, whilst unwelcome are regarded as a fact of life, unpleasant but not disastrous.

Britain is now governable not least because its people have both demanded new standards and accepted the new realism.

Amongst the secondary effects of Thatcherism has been the impact of these changes of attitude upon the country's second political party and only potential alternative government. Like the government of the Irish Republic which lives with the obvious lie of an avowed policy of having no territorial claim to Ulster alongside a constitution which contains an explicit claim to sovereignty over the whole island of Ireland, Labour is now forced to live with the lie of policies apparently accepting the capitalist market economy and a constitution binding it to state ownership, control and direction of industry and commerce. It would be foolish to believe that Mr Kinnock had undergone an intellectual conversion to capitalism. He is equipped neither emotionally nor intellectually to do so. He and his party managers have simply read the polls and listened to the voices telling them that Labour's former product has become unsaleable. In consequence Labour now claims to have a market orientated economic policy, rejecting 'old fashioned nationalisation', high taxation, state direction of industry and trades union power. Unhappily price control, some form of wage control, a 50 per cent increase in the tax on higher incomes, state intervention to 'improve' the performance of business and the removal of financial penalties on unlawful union activities are still on the agenda although re-packaged and re-labelled. The truth is that it is the packaging, not the policies which are market driven. Whatever might be the outcome if Labour were to achieve a majority in the House of Commons, its electoral proposition is an undertaking to no more change the Thatcherite status quo than Butler wanted to change the Labour status quo.

In short, Margaret Thatcher demonstrated that the ratchet effect could be put to good use. All that was needed – and what she provided – was the will power and skill to dismantle the ratchet and reassemble it to allow movement only to the right. Her success came where she was most radical. Her failures – the continuing growth of welfarism, the high cost/low productivity poor quality problems in the NHS and education – are in the areas where she was least radical or waited too long to begin her reforms.

Neither Britain nor the world are the same. Margaret Thatcher achieved more change for good than any of her predecessors. She is a Conservative in the line of Burke and Peel.

CHAPTER THREE

Foreign Policy

British foreign policy during the Thatcher administration has been more clearly founded on a clear assessment of what has been in the national interest than for many years past. In that process there has also been a more rational (some might say hard-headed) assessment of the real influence, let alone the moral standing and motives, of those who claim to speak for 'world opinion' whatever that may be. In short its genesis shares much in common with that of France, but where French foreign policy has become a byword for cynical shifts, deals and bad faith in pursuit of self-interest, British policy has operated in the belief that it is in the long-term national interest · to stand by allies, understandings, commitments and agreements through thick and thin despite short-term costs or disadvantages.

In that sense our foreign policy has been unusual although not unique, but it is certainly based on a history and present circumstances which are unique. Britain is set apart by a combination of circumstances which offer a package of challenges and opportunities not shared by any other nation. As a long-established independent nation, unconquered for more than 900 years with a record of almost uninterrupted progress towards democracy and even more unusual of progress to a state of individual liberty under law which pre-dated universal democratic rights, we are unique.

The British Empire was larger and lasted longer into modern times than any other. We are and long have been a world trading nation, which became industrialised earlier than any others. As a result of imperial conquest and trade, English language, culture, law and commercial practice are more widely spread than any others. Britain still carries the burdens (and some residual benefits) of the imperial past and most unusually shares language and cultural origins with our superpower ally and erstwhile colony, the United States of America, yet we are being increasingly integrated alongside our former enemies and allies in the European Community.

Perhaps Britain's foreign policy would have been easier to resolve had we not been divided by 3,000 miles of ocean from the nation with whom we have most in common and set cheek by jowel, only twenty miles from the mainland and the nations with whom since Roman times we have shared all too little save music and architecture except participation in two thousand years of bloody raiding and wars. In the post-war era, driven by fear of each other and of economic domination from outside Europe, the leading continental powers created the European Community from which we were originally self-excluded by Empire and a history of regretting mainland entanglements. At roughly the same time, fear of Marxist Russian imperialism led Britain, most European democratic powers, USA and Canada into the North Atlantic Treaty Organisation. More recently, fear of economic isolation and of being squeezed between the potentially protectionist American and European trading blocs, persuaded us into the EEC.

Whatever the errors or opportunities missed by post-war

British governments and our allies, when the post-war period is set against past experience it has been one of immense and unparalleled success. The economies of the warring nations of West Europe have been successfully rebuilt, democratic government has strengthened and grown, and former belligerents have integrated their economies and co-operated politically to an extent which makes renewed military war between them unthinkable. For that the Europeans owe a seldom acknowledged debt of gratitude to the wisdom and generosity of the United States as well as that more often expressed to the early post-war West European statesmen.

Just as sharp a discontinuity in the path of history has been achieved by the foresight and fortitude of American, British and continental democratic leaders who conceived, built and maintained the North Atlantic Alliance. The preservation of freedom and the avoidance of European and intercontinental wars for almost fifty years owes little to the babbling polyglot hypocrisy upon which the United Nations habitually nourishes itself and everything to the Western alliances and their influence.

In retrospect it is easy to mark the post-war settlement of 1945 between the Axis and Western powers, the creation of the European Community and of NATO as marking a decisive break with the past cycle of post-war settlements which became the breeding ground of subsequent wars. It is less easy to be sure that such changes are indeed permanent and universal. There never was, nor perhaps can be, any certainty that the world may not regress into its old bad habits, or that new bad habits will not constantly threaten to establish themselves unnoticed or at least tolerated or ignored for too long.

For the past forty-five years the principal threat to the new order has been from Marxist imperialism – most notably Russian-based but for a while Chinese too. In the early post-war period the Western alliance was sufficiently robust to face and

37

defeat aggressive probing by the Soviet Union and China. Through those years the United States' willingness to commit military forces to action in Korea and Vietnam, as well as the readiness to outface the USSR in Western Europe, and in the Cuban missiles crisis, as well as to maintain for decades the heavy burden of nuclear determent, not only contained the Marxist powers but placed an ever-growing burden of military cost on the Soviet Union. It can now be seen that the growing cost of military spending and the steady deterioration of its socialist economy forced the Soviet political establishment to change tactics if not strategy in the 1980s. Quite contrary to Moscow's hopes (and probably to their expectations) the election of President Reagan and Mrs Thatcher strengthened the determination of the West to maintain the military strength of the West. The Campaign for Nuclear Disarmament and the various front organisations sympathetic to Marxist organisations lost rather than gained ground in Britain, which is the European hinge upon which NATO hangs.

The Falklands war was quite outside the East-West conflict and the cold war but had an important effect upon it. It demonstrated the resolution of Mrs Thatcher's government in protecting British interests, the competence of our armed forces, and the strength of the Anglo-American alliance – particularly the willingness of President Reagan to risk United States objectives in Latin America to support his British ally. That loyalty was well repaid with British support for the American Strategic Defense Initiative (SDI or 'Star Wars') and the European deployment of US cruise missiles in response to Russia's SS20s targeted on European cities. The hysteria generated by misguided but genuine peace-lovers as well as the front organisations and the fellow travellers within various 'peace groups' has now faded from memory, but at the time it heavily infected the Labour Party and important parts of the media. Even some normally balanced and reasonable people gave some credence to the Soviet propagandists' line that SDI was a preparation for a pre-emptive strike against Russia and that the European deployment of cruise missiles was a possibly irrevocable step towards nuclear war. In addition, many people believed scare-mongering pseudo-environmental groups who concocted wild tales of the possibility of missiles being accidentally triggered by road accidents involving the mobile launchers upon which they were mounted.

It is not inconceivable that even a Conservative government under a different leadership than that of Mrs Thatcher might have buckled under such pressure. It is entirely inconceivable that, in the mood of the Labour Party at that time, a Labour government would not have caved in.

In the event Mrs Thatcher's government supported President Reagan on both issues and by doing so enabled some at least of the mainland NATO allies to follow suit. But for Britain's leadership Chancellor Kohl would certainly not have been able to overcome the resistance of Germany's powerful left wing, pacifist and green lobbies to deploy Cruise in Germany. The Soviet Union would then have achieved a huge military advantage and political success by driving a wedge between the United States and its European allies. Since US troops would have lacked effective nuclear deterrence the domestic US pressure for their withdrawal would have grown, pushing the administration towards a 'Fortress USA' policy of sheltering behind the defensive SDI screen and overwhelming intercontinental nuclear capability.

The Soviet political response to SDI was led by a successful misinformation campaign to undermine the credibility of the concept. However, the Russians sought to make the cancellation of SDI a pre-condition of arms reduction talks thus suggesting they believed that SDI would give the United States a decisive advantage. That view may well have been based on the results of their own work on a similar scheme. Although successful deployment of such a system must always have been subject to the uncertainties inherent in such an advanced project, there was no doubt that costs would be huge, almost certainly more than Russia, or perhaps even the United States, could afford.

In short the determination of NATO, which hinged upon that of Mrs Thatcher, was imposing economic costs which though uncomfortable in the capitalist West were simply unsupportable in the socialist East, and the Soviet Union had to change tactics. The clear failure of policy, and the huge costs of military spending crushing the ramshackle socialist economies of the Eastern bloc, broke the grip of the reactionary hardliners and brought a new group into power.

At the same time the patriotic nationalist and anti-Marxist forces in the Warsaw Pact satellite states were so encouraged and strengthened by the disarray in the Kremlin as to overthrow the Moscow-backed dictatorships.

It is still too early to say if the economic liberals and democrats led or were used by the new Soviet establishment, or if the new men will hold on to power against the hatred of the old guard and the disillusionment of the people. The cold war may not yet be over – indeed, it may intensify as the old guard regain power and seek to regain lost ground – but the West has won an important if not decisive battle in the long struggle between the democratic and the socialist forces.

During 1991 the Soviet economy deteriorated further and it became clear that Mr Gorbachev's supporters whilst talking of a market economy are still unable to make the intellectual leap from the centrally managed system of socialism to a liberal capitalist one. The need of Western aid may yet force reform but nothing is yet certain.

Whatever the outcome of the power struggle within the Soviet Union, Mr Gorbachev's foreign policy during the Gulf crisis was certainly very different to that which might have been expected during the time of Mr Brezhnev. It is possible to argue that had Brezhnev been in power Saddam Hussein would never have been allowed to commit the folly of his attack upon Kuwait. Be that as it may, Mr Gorbachev's acceptance of the legitimacy of the Allied military response spearheaded by American forces was a dramatic and hopeful change from Russia's cold war stance. In opening up the prospect of a more constructive period in which the two superpowers would seek common ground in dealing with incidents such as the invasion of Kuwait, Mr Gorbachev has given the world some reason for cautious optimism about the future. It is a far cry from the Berlin airlift, the Cuban missiles crisis, Vietnam and the invasion of Afghanistan. As yet it would be wise to assume that the new policy is no more deeply rooted than Mr Gorbachev, but if it became firmly entrenched in the post-Gorbachev era it would then be time for a major Western reassessment of policies and attitudes.

Nearer to home, foreign policy has revolved around the European Community.

Membership of the Community may be in our best economic interest but it is bound to be uncomfortable. Britain has no more to gain and much more to lose by membership than our partners. Of the other eleven only Spain, Portugal, France and the Netherlands have an established history of nationhood. Every one of them, bar Ireland, has experienced dictatorship, civil war or foreign military occupation within living memory. Almost without exception our partners are by instinct corporatist and protectionist, bedevilled by excessive regulation made tolerable only by a well established tradition of massive public non-compliance. We have long taken the view that the law belongs to the individual citizen as much as to the state. We have for many years taken pride in a legal system which can be invoked by the citizen against the state as well as by the state against the citizen. There has been a long British tradition of a judiciary independent of both the executive and the legislature. Such ideas, even where present on the continent are in their infancy.

Our partners are each governed under the latest version of written and in many cases much re-written constitutions of post-war origin. In contrast our own constitution, whilst it is not unwritten, is not contained in any single document but within numerous statutes dating back to Magna Carta at least, conventions and established rights which precede even that, countless legal judgments under statute and common law and undertakings made in or to Parliament. Far older and more complex than continental constitutions, ours is both more enduring yet more able to undergo incremental change than the brittle modern constructions of our mainland partners. Quite rightly the people of those countries have no undue attachment to, nor respect for, their ephemeral constitutions which in historical terms are put on or cast off to suit the political climate of the century or more often the decade.

For our partners the British attachment to what they see as outdated forms and abstractions is sentimental insular reactionaryism. To us it is an unspoken acknowledgement of the cumulative experience of unbroken centuries of successful self-government. They see constitutions the way Americans see motor cars – part of the utilitarian throw-away society, and feel no sense of loss, nor guilt of betrayal, when they allow the superimposition of Brussels law over that of their own callow legislatures.

The liberty and democratic systems of most of our partners have been either rescued by, or imposed under, foreign military power and they cannot comprehend that we enjoyed liberty before democracy or that we achieved both for ourselves without foreign intervention. They mostly cannot distinguish between what is patriotism and what is nationalism but have come to vaguely characterise the one as benign and the other malign. The British, or perhaps more accurately the English, have long been infused with patriotism but have no real sense of nationalism as it has manifested itself in Germany or France. Our nearest equivalent to that is the degraded drunken antics of soccer yobs and hooligans.

Much of these differences spring from the good fortune of having long enjoyed frontiers (that troublesome one in Ireland excepted) made and left unchanged for aeons by God, Providence or geology rather than made and unmade in every post-war settlement by the politicians and generals of the day. Within the European Common Market into which the United Kingdom entered in 1972 these differences could be contained. Each partner retained its own cherished or variously valued sovereignty; that is not just the ability of the state to assert its right to act unilaterally if needs be in its own self-interest, but the right of its people to self-determination and self-government. In those circumstances the difference in quality of national institutions and the esteem in which they were held was not a cross-border issue.

Sadly the European Common Market or Economic Community has been superseded by the European Community in which member states concede far greater powers to be used in common by a central authority. Even this is now under threat of being overtaken by the vision of political, economic and monetary union – that is, the Euro State in which the central authority has powers by right and a sovereignty of its own – and only by grace and at its discretion allows subsidiary matters to be dealt with by devolved government at the level of former national governments.

The Common Market was a market, each part of which was managed under agreed non-discriminatory rules by the national governments, and made fully open to use by each of the partners. Only the United Kingdom observed either the law or the spirit of that concept, as successive British governments –

above all that of Mrs Thatcher – struggled to achieve it more widely. Progress was slow. The corporatists and protectionists had little interest in the liberal British concept of an open and free Common Market and, however good the intentions of those operating in Brussels, national governments frustrated its operation. Uniquely in Britain, even had a Government sought to renege on its undertakings to its partners, the British judicial system could and was used to enforce compliance.

If Britain was not to be constantly cheated by its partners the United Kingdom had no choice but either to repudiate the Treaty and leave the Common Market or to find a new way forward. Leaving the Community was thought to be unthinkable, and a new initiative was sought. It crystallized as the creation of the Single Market to replace the Common Market. Unhappily that has changed the Community from one in which power or sovereignty was distributed to one in which it is being centralised. The Common Market 'belonged' to the signatory nations of the Treaty of Rome. The Single Market essentially 'belongs' to the central authority – today a mixture of the Council and the Commission, with the Parliament ever more eager to take powers from national parliaments to itself.

The British view was, and to a large extent still is, that that was all rather theoretical and having conceded some powers to the centre that was that. We had found a sensible mechanism to pressurise our partners to deliver what they had undertaken. The view of our partners seemed to be that insofar as they would deliver (and so far that is not very much) it would be worth it. They had, in their view, got Britain on the slippery slope from nationhood and self-government towards provincial states within a supranational system.

Sir Geoffrey Howe was undoubtedly sincere when he told the House of Commons (23 April 1986):

I know that there are some who will be anxious that in

promoting the achievement of an internal market in this way we may diminish the essential protection of our national interest that is inherent in the requirement for unanimity [in voting in the Council of Ministers]. I would not accept that: first, because we have got the safeguards that I have described, which protect us on the key issues; secondly, because it will be open to us to combine with other members states to form a blocking minority; and, thirdly, because, as a last resort, the Luxembourg compromise remains in place untouched and unaffected ... The one thing that is clear is that the Luxembourg compromise as I have described it is in no way affected one way or the other by the Single European Act ...

No doubt the House will hear a good deal from some of my hon. Friends and from some Opposition Members about the fearful constitutional fantasies that preoccupy them. Those are terrors for children; not for me. I hope that the House will put them aside ...

His Minister of State, Lynda Chalker, was equally clear when she dismissed the worries of Members of Parliament:

What the Single European Act will not do – and I think it is worth emphasising this – is that it will not lead to a federal union, which is so much feared by the hon. Member for Walthamstow [Mr Deakin] ...

Several hon. Members were, not for the first time, excited because they believe that the Bill will remove the United Kingdom's power of veto, give greater powers to the European Parliament and reduce the role of other institutions. I am afraid that those opponents of the Bill are allowing themselves to be drawn into an unreal world ... I shall deal first with the Luxembourg compromise ...

We did not lightly agree to move from the veto inherent in unanimity to the lack of an absolute treaty-based veto inherent in qualified majority voting. That was why the treaty changes are limited to those areas where majority voting will serve our long-standing objective – the completion of the internal market. That is why we have retained essential safeguards for small and medium-sized businesses and in health matters. In these circumstances, the Luxembourg compromise is an additional, but not our principal, safeguard. It is not affected by the Bill.

Much of that is now in doubt. Our partners interpreted matters very differently. So how did such a huge decision come to be taken with so little debate?

In retrospect it is clear that the complex nature of modern government and the proliferation of Cabinet committees and sub-committees has reinforced the tendency of Ministers to look after the affairs of their own departments and to contribute less and less to any open general discussion of great issues. Nor did Mrs Thatcher's mastery of both the principles and the details of every issue encourage Cabinet Ministers to devote any less time to the details of their departmental affairs or any more to the questioning of the judgement of their colleagues. As a result, the Cabinet considered the issue of the Single Market and the Single European Act only from the British point of view, never seeing that the signals it gave to our partners were wholly different to those intended by the Prime Minister – though not necessarily wholly different to those intended by the eternally defeatist Foreign Office.

Nor did Parliament wake up to the significance of the change from Common to Single Market, or the political as opposed to the legal significance of the Single European Act. Sadly the small vociferous anti-EEC group of MPs had used up their credibility and were unheeded when they sounded the alarm. Sadly the ability of Parliament to identify and debate the big issues of policy seems to have diminished as it has disintegrated into huddles of myopic 'specialist' departmental select committees seeking out what they call the 'nitty gritty' of politics. In consequence the select committees have become dominated by narrow-minded single-issue politics (a contradiction in terms but no better term exists) and by specialist advisers with bees in their bonnets. The profession of politics may have its detractors but I find politicians who become 'monoticians' even less attractive than I do those who allow their proliferating 'research assistants' to lead them by the nose into backwaters of politics made stagnant by wearisome bogs of statistics and discussion papers through which no river of thought is ever likely to penetrate.

Fortunately some issues, such as policy towards South Africa, had become so polarised, others such as that of the Hong Kong settlement with China were dictated remorselessly by the facts of power and self-interest, and those of the Falklands and Kuwait arose so swiftly that there was no time for the process of obfuscation of the main question with mountains of peripheral and secondary matters.

As a result British interests in each of these areas were effectively pursued. In South Africa the British, or perhaps one should say the Thatcher policy is being proved right. In Hong Kong it has generally been so with the exception of the lamentable offer to grant United Kingdom passports to some 250,000 ethnic Chinese.

In that instance the Thatcher government yielded to a skilful public relations campaign and put at risk its own promise to end large-scale immigration, its good relations with China and the future of Hong Kong. Fortunately it seems that most Hong Kong Chinese may have a clearer view of their best interests than their spokesmen or the British Government and have elected already either to leave the Colony or to stay under Chinese rule without the disadvantage of foreign nationality.

The Falklands affair held numerous lessons. It was significant that the United States, despite sharp divisions within the administration over where the prime American interest lay, gave more support (and at greater diplomatic cost in Latin America) than our European partners. Indeed, as in the Kuwait crisis some eight years later, the partnership between the United States and Great Britain yielded more than that between the United States and its other allies or Britain and its European or Commonwealth partners.

Where then in the last decade of the century should United Kingdom foreign policy be leading?

Without question the United Kingdom must have a foreign policy independent of the United States and the European Community. That is not to say that the general thrust of policy will necessarily differ from that of either our principal ally nor those of our principal partners. However, within that general consensus the British interest will frequently differ, and it will pay to maintain an ability to 'trade' UK support for what others may want in areas where our interest is not at stake, for support in areas in which it is.

There is no evidence to suggest a likelihood of any widespread outbreak of a universal spirit of the brotherhood of man, peace and justice. The welcome collapse of the capacity of the Soviet Union to enlarge either its empire or its sphere of influence or to impose its political and economic system on others has made the world a safer but not a safe place – and that only if the democratic Western and Pacific powers have the ability and purposefulness to exploit the opportunities and to guard against the dangers now presenting themselves.

There is a very real danger that as America sees the power of the Soviet Union waning and becomes convinced that neither it, nor Western Europe, is under military threat, the pressure to reduce its troublesome budgetary and trade deficits by withdrawing its forces from Europe will grow. The response of the European democratic powers should be to increase the contribution which they make to the defence of their own continent and their own countries. Britain carries a disproportionate defence burden in relation to the size of our economy and must trim back rather than increase its defence expenditure, and there is little sign of our partners being willing to raise their spending towards our levels. The prospect is therefore for a considerable long-term weakening of the ability to defend Europe unless NATO uses its current advantage over the Soviet Union to force deep cuts in the Russian forces.

The efforts of our partners to extend Community competence to defence and foreign policy is highly dangerous and quite unacceptable. The inability of the Community to take difficult decisions in a timely manner was well demonstrated during the 1990 negotiations in the GATT round of world trade talks in which it already enjoys competence. It should have come as no surprise that a coalition of coalitions should be weak, indecisive and a prey to short-term opportunism. Nor was the display of disunity, cowardice, narrow self-interest and plain weakness of will and resolve during the Gulf crisis any more reassuring.

The Euro fanatics would have us believe that it would all be well if we consigned our national rights in foreign policy and defence to a 'real' European government comprising an executive drawn from the Commission and to a European Parliament with enhanced powers to form a legislature and a check and balance on the executive. All experience suggests that polyglot parliaments are unlikely to succeed. National or regional interests are too strong and there can be no prospect of the creation of a European public opinion (akin to that of the USA) for many, many years if ever. Without such a unifying force the Parliament would be unable to make effective use of its powers and would be a cockpit of shifty dealing between the vote-brokers in unmanageable and constantly shifting coalitions. Britain's interest (and indeed that of the other European powers

49

within and without the European Community) would be best served by the present multinational relationship within NATO. The alternative would be for Britain to be represented by a spokesman representing a lowest common denominator of agreement within the Community which had been reached without regard to the relative military contributions of the partners but taking account of the neutralist stance of Ireland. The other European NATO members, Turkey and Norway, would inevitably be somewhat sidelined.

It is difficult enough at times to accept that the British Trade Secretary should be excluded from any part in negotiations about our own trade but to allow the Secretary of State for Defence to be locked out of discussions within NATO, or for Britain's vote in the Security Council to be cast on the say-so of a majority over-ruling the British, would be simply unacceptable.

The first essential of our policy must therefore be to maintain the existing structure of NATO and the maximum commitment of the USA whilst encouraging the other European nations to accept a fairer share of the burden of defence which provides their security.

That does not detract from the value of the European Community as a forum within which, or on 'the fringes' of which, discussions can take place between friendly partners seeking to find a common viewpoint on policy or on such matters as defence procurement. Ever closer relationships will naturally lead to such things and it is entirely sensible that should be so, but the discussions and deals should be between sovereign nations.

The one certainty over the next decade is the uncertainty brought about by the collapse of the Soviet Empire which has left great instability in its wake. Had the Russian socialist system brought great prosperity to accompany the centralised authoritarian government, the Empire might well have lasted for many decades to come. But contrary to those who believe the anti-Soviet revolution is inspired by economic factors alone and that nationalism is merely the froth on the turbulence, it is nationalism which is the force destroying the Soviet Empire and economic failure which has triggered the revolution, not the other way around. Nowhere is this better demonstrated than in the break up of Yugoslavia, which is a further reminder that people will not consent to be ruled by those who do not speak their language.

Further economic collapse and the threat of anarchy could lead either to a counter-revolution and a socialist military dictatorship or a break-up into separate nations. Either way there are clear dangers, whether Soviet military power becomes widely dissipated with the frightening prospect of civil wars or further concentrated by the generals holding both political and military power.

NATO with its tactical strategic nuclear capability, backed by the United States' naval and air power, is the only credible counter to the dangers of civil war spreading out of the Soviet Union or adventurism by a military government unrestrained by civilian control. It must therefore remain a priority of British defence and foreign policy to preserve that organisation. That carries with it the unspoken but well understood obligation of the United Kingdom to understand and to support wherever possible our principal ally diplomatically and, when appropriate, militarily when its vital interests are at stake. Needless to say that requires that our foreign and defence policy must be independent and whilst it must take into account the powerful influence of our mutual economic interests within the European Community they must not override that imperative.

Membership of both NATO and the European Community (subject to the dangers discussed later in this chapter) are at the heart of Britain's foreign policy. Far less so is membership of the Commonwealth. It would be foolish to give gratuitous offence to our fellow members of that ghost from our imperial past but it is easy to argue that neither the United Kingdom nor the wider world would lose much if it ceased to exist. The country-to-country ties of the old Commonwealth have greatly weakened. Canada has cut off itself from Britain and is bound to become more and more interdependent upon its neighbour, the USA. Indeed if the linguistic and cultural stresses within Canada become too powerful to contain the French nationalism of Quebec, severing that province from its Anglophone partners, then they would be almost bound to integrate fully with America. Ties have been similarly weakened as the ethnic composition of Australia has changed but cultural and business influences remain strong in both directions. New Zealand, too, small to generate an industrial economy, cut off from its natural British markets for agricultural products, remains more ethnically and culturally British and both deserves and needs British support. In much of the rest of the Commonwealth the British ideals of Westminster-style democratic government and honest administration have failed to take root, though no one can fail to be impressed by the remarkable achievements of India in preserving democracy for so long against extraordinary ethnic, religious, linguistic and economic difficulties although the future now looks doubtful. Malaysia, too, has pursued similar ideals through similar difficulties and Singapore has successfully survived as a mini-nation state against all the odds. Whilst neither the record nor prospects of the black African states are encouraging there is hope that some settlement preserving an orderly and prosperous South Africa may emerge to give a prospect of extending those most desirable attributes northwards.

In short the Commonwealth is a club of such disparate states that its long-term survival must be in doubt. It must come a poor third in importance to NATO and the European Community but it is worth preserving provided it costs Britain nothing (and that means a more rigorous attitude towards immigration) and within it there are important bilateral relationships.

Despite all its shortcomings and serious faults the United Nations exists, and if it did not, some such organisation would have to be invented. Although a new United Nations might (but only might) be shorn of some of the hypocrisy, bureaucracy and extravagance of the present organisation it would be unlikely to feature a Security Council structure so sensible or so advantageous to our interest. We would be wise therefore to accept the United Nations warts and all, rather than either to leave it or to attempt a major reconstruction. Equally, we would be foolish to seek to increase its power or indeed influence since by the very 'one member, one vote' constitution of the General Assembly the democratic nations are always potentially at risk.

The coalition of nations supporting Kuwait against Iraqi aggression used the United Nations very skilfully and the United Nations resolutions gave cover, and some would say legitimacy, to the use of force against the aggressor. It would be dangerous, however, to imply that Britain accepted either that the use of force is always legitimate if authorised by the United Nations or that it could never be legitimate without such authorisation. The Gulf War rhetoric came too close at times to carrying such an implication and it would be helpful if before too long Britain made it quite plain that whilst UN support for action in the Gulf was welcome it was not essential nor would its absence have constituted a veto.

It may be that the alliance between Western and a wide range of Arab powers which formed the coalition during the Gulf War, and the skilful use of the United Nations set a precedent which could be used to make progress with the problems of Israel, her Arab citizens and her neighbours. Had Saddam Hussein not stupidly attacked Israel with Scud missiles, Israel would not have been able to earn plaudits and potential favours for its self-restraint – which was in reality self-interest.

That glimmer of hope had been all but extinguished within six months by the complete intransigence of Mr Shamir towards any proposed solution except on terms dictated by Israel and his weakness towards, or encouragement of, the illegal Israeli settlement of the occupied territories. None the less, there has been a demonstration of the use of predominantly Western military power with the consent of the Soviet Union to protect a small state against aggression. Of course if Israel were to be overwhelmed, aid would have to come more swiftly than it did to Kuwait, a fact used by Israel to justify its continuing occupation of another state's territory as a forward defensive line.

However, the price of aggression, indeed of war, has been well displayed in Iraq and Kuwait to Arab and Jew alike. It may just be that President Bush could find enough political muscle, especially in a second term, to overcome the Jewish lobby and cut back aid to Israel unless the provocation of illegal settlement ended and a more genuine effort was made to reach an understanding with her neighbours.

The key regional power is undoubtedly Syria and although its regime is far from attractive it has acted more responsibly of late and may have concluded that the de-escalation of the superpower conflict has robbed it of its most powerful weapon, leaving little option but to seek an accord.

Britain can do little until the United States is more willing to use its economic power – or to be more brutal about it – to resist the emotional (and electoral) blackmail of Israel. Our policy should be to support Israel's right to a secure independence since she, as a democratic and economically efficient power, is both a potential ally and force for good in an unstable and economically undeveloped region, but to work for a compromise underwritten by political and military guarantees. Mr Shamir is not the best man to make the case against negotiation with terrorist organisations even if they have renounced violence, but we should be cautious of legitimising the PLO whilst it uses terror tactics against moderate Palestinians. Again that points to Damascus as the likeliest place in which deals might be made and it is time that the relationship between Syria and Britain was improved to that end.

If the superpower rivalry in the Middle East really is at an end, the self-interests of all governments will be to find a settlement in the interests of their economies and to avoid war, hot or cold. That will tend to reduce the power of the hardline Palestinian lobby in the Arab capitals and of the hardline Jewish lobby in America. Although the pernicious proportional representation system in Israel gives the extreme hardliners excessive power to prevent any settlement, there is at least a chance that combined Western and Soviet pressure could open a path for compromise – and Britain should have an active role in seeking its achievement.

The Gulf War, like the Falklands campaign, illustrated clearly why Britain must maintain both a military capability to operate well outside the confines of Europe or NATO and the political will to match. However, our interests are usually better served by rather less expensive and destructive methods. Our diplomacy should be based on our interests in a peaceful, orderly, prosperous and preferably domestic world. Trade is overwhelmingly important to us, more so in general than any desire to interfere in the internal affairs of other nations. If that was not the case we would do much more interfering and a lot less trading with undemocratic and inefficient third world countries. However, where countries seek economic aid unless some vital British interest or overwhelming humanitarian need takes precedence, it should be granted only provided the recipient government follows sensible economic policies. We remain a major aid donor, giving far more in any terms than many of the nations who criticise us and we should expect that aid to be truly beneficial in the longer term to the recipient nations. Even so, trade is more important than aid, and the ending of the European Community's inefficient, expensive, wasteful and selfish agricultural policy would do more for both the East European nations and third world economies (and European consumers) than any aid programme. That should remain a priority of British policy.

Overall the experience of the last forty-five years, and the Thatcher years in particular, should persuade us that self-interest and the capacity for self-protection, combined with loyalty to the allies and institutions which have served us well, are the only pillars upon which foreign policy may prudently be built.

CHAPTER FOUR

The European Community and the British Constitution

Reference is made elsewhere in this book to the inherent conflict between the continental and British attitudes towards nationhood, nationality and government. It is a conflict well illustrated by the wise words of Lord Hailsham in his autobiography *A Sparrow's Flight*:

> Human institutions are of two kinds, the traditional and the contrived. Most partake of some elements of each, with one or the other predominating. The Papacy and the British Monarchy are obvious examples of the traditional; the German Federal Republic and the Soviet Union are examples of the latter. The difference resides in the fact that, whilst everyone knows that no human institution lasts forever, and that every long-standing institution develops its own customary ethos, contrived institutions look for intellectual justification in terms of the ideologies at the time of their creation whilst the traditional are judged by the extent to which they are considered useful in society now. The one question is 'How well does it work?'

Our legal and constitutional arrangements have for many years been under assault not only from well-intentioned reformers but all manner of quacks and charlatans peddling cures for the perceived constitutional troubles of the day. This is not always an entirely negative process since it raises not only Lord Hailsham's question 'Does it work?' but 'Could it be made to work better?' and may well be a force for useful change – even if not along the lines the quacks and zealots might wish.

However, by nature and almost without exception, the kinds of change initially proposed are of the contrived variety devised by idealogues. In recent years the home-grown end of this pressure (as opposed to the Brussels end) has been well exemplified by the Charter 88 Group. Unsurprisingly many of the signatories to this proposed Charter are foreigners seemingly obsessed with the desire to make Britain more like the countries from which they have fled. Amongst the nostrums of Charter 88 are a written constitution, entrenched to make amendment or parliamentary override extremely difficult, and proportional representation.

The advocates of a written or contrived constitution pour scorn on Britain's diffuse, flexible and enduring constitution, arguing that it offers insufficient rights and protection to women, racial and religious minorities and deviant sexual groups, amongst others. Only an entrenched constitution, they argue, would be proof against what its advocates regard as the risk of a capricious election result allowing the people to amend or even overthrow it. One only has to consider the status such an entrenched constitution might have awarded women, coloured people, non-Christians or sexual deviants had it been written in, say, 1910 or 1920 to realise that the enthusiasts for written constitutions are almost without exception overwhelmingly arrogant. They cannot imagine that any social structure which did not accord with their ephemeral prejudices could be popular, acceptable or morally defensible. Yet of its

Edmund Burke, the father of Conservative philosophy. The essence of what he wrote in the eighteenth century was the essence of Conservatism's most successful period for a hundred years, the Thatcher administration of 1979 to 1990.
(National Portrait Gallery)

Robert Peel, the father of the Conservative Party. Peel's economic views brought him into sharp dispute with the Tory paternalists in a confrontation much like that of the Wet versus Dry struggle of the 1980s.
(Hulton-Deutsch Collection)

Harold Macmillan, an unrepentant corporatist – but was he a Conservative?
(Weidenfeld and Nicolson Archive)

RIGHT: *The Falkland Islands, April 1982. British Falklander children watch invading Argentinian troop carriers go past. The Falklands war demonstrated the resolution of Mrs Thatcher's Government, the competence of our armed forces and the strength of the Anglo-American alliance.*
(Spooner/Gamma)

President Gorbachev. The Cold War may not yet be over but the West has won an important battle in the long struggle between the forces of democracy and those of socialism.
(Spooner/Gamma)

The Berlin Wall, 1989. NATO's determination to resist Soviet imperialism imposed unsupportable military costs on the Soviet Union and led to the overthrow of socialist governments in the Warsaw Pact states.
(Impact/Odyssey)

The General Assembly of the United Nations. UN support for action in the Gulf was welcome but not essential.
(UN Photo)

RIGHT: *Mrs Thatcher arrives for a Brussels summit in 1982.* (Spooner/Gamma)

Jacques Delors, now President of the European Commission, with other Finance Ministers of the Community in 1983. His ambitions to create a Euro-superstate put at risk the European Community itself. (Spooner/Gamma)

British Steel – almost without exception privatised businesses have achieved the success which eluded them in state ownership.
(British Steel)

Pickets and police clash during the 1984–5 miners' strike. No leader except Mrs Thatcher would have had the courage to fight this dispute through to victory.
(John Arthur/Impact)

LEFT: *Uncollected rubbish in Liverpool. In 1979 Liverpool's problems were typical of Britain's, but by 1990 only Liverpool remained locked in the world of the 1970s.*
(Philip Gordon/Impact)

Pupils at a school in Nottingham. Despite the investment made in education there is overwhelming evidence of falling standards.
(Adam Hinton/Impact)

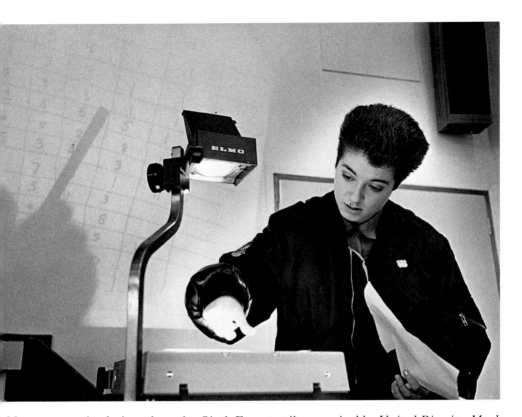

Management-simulation scheme for Sixth Form pupils, organised by United Biscuits. Much more needs to be done – including sponsorship – to persuade universities to listen to market signals.
(Andrew Moore/Impact)

Young YTS decorators in South Wales. The beginnings of wider vocational training for young school-leavers.
(Anita Corbin/Impact)

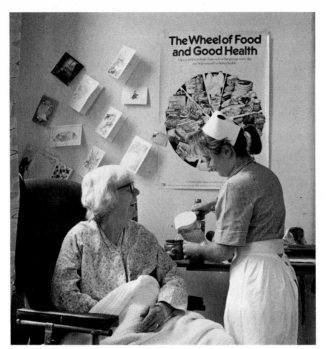

LEFT: *A patient at King's College Hospital, London. The demand for medicine increases, with no limits yet in sight. Sooner or later, hard choices will have to be made.*
(David Lurie/Impact)

1987 – celebrating three in a row.
(Press Association)

kind, among major nations only the American constitution has lasted more than half a century and few have yet been stressed by changing moral and social standards. The constitution of the Irish Republic should stand as a terrible warning. Its claim to sovereignty over Ulster is now the main obstacle to a peaceful settlement of a centuries-old dispute. The government of the Republic and the main opposition parties are agreed that the people of Ulster are entitled to self-determination, yet like rabbits facing a stoat they contemplate a constitution which requires their courts to allow terrorists to go unpunished since they dare not legislate to amend it.

The constitutional meddlers are concerned also to reform the House of Lords. In my judgement any substantial reform would be a mistake. In general, bicameral legislatures work quite well and rather better than single chambers, and in Britain our system has grown around an assumption of twin chambers, in which one is the clear master but the other maintains an important role. Few practical politicians would advocate an elected second chamber, for it would naturally claim to represent the people with equal legitimacy to that of the first. Without a written constitution, with all its horrors, especially if we continued to draw our executive from and base it within the legislature, two elected chambers would be a recipe for constant argument not only over the merits of any decision but over which had the right to make it. The present system of a House comprising a very large membership (over 750 hereditary and 370 life peers and peeresses), with a normal working group of regular attenders of some 350, works very well indeed. Whatever the subject of debate there are peers who are expert or experienced in the field. In addition, as the Lords lacks any retirement age and on the whole peers inherit at a mature age with life peerages tending also to be awarded in later life, the consensus of the House is likely to be twenty years or so out of phase with that of the Commons. That is a valuable check and balance against the elected Commons rushing headlong into either so-called progressive or reactionary legislation and although the elected House will always have its way, delay and amendment often avoid or soften the impact of fashionable follies.

It has been interesting to see how in the time of the unhealthy consensus of Butskellism, the Lords often spoke for the more traditional Conservative view and during the Thatcher ascendancy it has frequently upheld obsolete Butskellism and the corporatism of the Wilson-Heath period. No doubt as the Thatcherites retire from the Commons to join the life peers of Mrs Thatcher's time in office the tone of debates in the Lords will change, even if (hopefully) that of those in the Commons may not.

The other principal call of the constitutional meddlers is for proportional representation. Such people are usually either supporters of parties or views which fail to find sufficient support to gain election under the present first-past-the-post or winner-takes-all system, or those anxious to prevent another party from winning a majority in the Commons and forming a government. The hallmark of the latter group is lack of confidence either in their advocacy of their own case or in the ability of the electors to make a sensible decision. Both groups are, in Lord Hailsham's terminology, contrivers and they ignore experience.

After all, the principal countries with histories of unbroken democratic rule without extremism for more than half a century (most notably the United States and the United Kingdom) have achieved them without proportional representation. On the other hand Hitler was first elected under a proportional representation system and Israel is prevented from finding any rapprochement with its neighbours not only by the intransigence of some of them but the intransigence which is built in to every Israeli government by the excessive power proportional representation gives to the tiny number of extreme religious and racial zealots. Of course proportional representation may well have a role in immature democracies. In South Africa, it might well be part of the mechanism needed to prevent a majority party from persecuting the minorities and to avoid a powerful and decisive national administration overriding the interests of the individual states.

The British system allows considerable power to be concentrated at the centre – as was the case during Britain's postwar socialist and corporatist periods or to be devolved, as it was by Mrs Thatcher by deregulation, denationalisation, limitation of taxation and transfer of power from quangos and town halls to individuals or market-responsive organisations.

The most likely constitutional changes now in prospect are within local government. In his March 1991 statement concerning local government structure and finance Mr Heseltine made up an entirely new and quite false constitutional theory, when he said: 'We need responsible elected local authorities *not only* to provide a check and balance to Westminster ...'

That is not true. Local government is not to be used or seen as a way of frustrating the outcome of general elections. It has only those powers given to it for the time being by Parliament, which is itself the main check and balance upon central government. Above all it has no rights of its own to tax and certainly not to do so in order to check or balance the tax policies of Parliament. In general we suffer from too much government – especially local government – and too little effective management and delivery of essential public services. The proper functions of local government are best looked at under two main headings, those functions which need local democratic accountability, planning for example, and others which do not.

Education no more needs local political control than does the provision of groceries. Indeed there is very good reason for saying it should not be controlled politically, but like the provision of food should be controlled by its consumers, or, in this case, their parents. Parents are in the overwhelming majority of cases as well able to choose schools for the children as they are to choose supermarkets for their groceries, houses, holidays, cars or shares to buy. The essential of universal free education is that the state should finance children at school – not choose their schools. It seems particularly odd to me that many of the same people who espouse the right of unmarried, perhaps sexually deviant, women to give birth to children (sometimes artificially at the expense of both taxpayers and those awaiting much needed medical treatment) and by design to raise them without a father, oppose most bitterly the right of normal mature parents to choose a school for their child.

A suitable structure for a depoliticised market responsive state financed education system is described in Chapter 6.

There are other services provided by local government where individual consumer choice would be difficult to arrange but delivery of which is not dependent upon, nor assisted by, being controlled by local politicians. Refuse collection, street lighting and maintenance are amongst those springing to mind. The minimum service levels might be set nationally by the needs of public health and safety and both the cost and any provisions above that by elected councillors. The delivery is, however, entirely a management task best carried out through a competitive tendering process. Indeed it is interesting that although the Labour Party are opposed to such a view in general, Mr Kinnock advocates it as the solution in part to the problems caused by Labour rule in the showcase of Labour government – Liverpool.

The growth of home ownership has greatly reduced the need for local authority housing and the recreation of a competitive rented sector would take that process further. No doubt tendering for the supply of special needs accommodation could be developed and the local authority housing function thus minimised. It is probably too much to hope that the provision of personal social services could be entirely arranged in the same manner.

The powers and obligations to protect children and other vulnerable groups currently exercised by local authorities should be subject to a process of democratic accountability. So, too, should regulatory tasks including consumer protection (the weights and measures inspectorate for example) and the exercise of planning controls. In their anxiety to create a local socialist municipal economy many Labour councils, not just Liverpool, neglect precisely these functions as the appalling scandal of cruelty in Staffordshire children's homes and the Hackney housing scandal illustrate.

The expected reform of local government into predominantly single tier authorities (with parish councils where appropriate) would offer a good opportunity to redefine the responsibilities and powers of local authorities hopefully distinguishing between management (best kept away from local politicians) and regulation and protection which demand democratic accountability. No doubt something of this was in the mind of Mr Heseltine when he floated the idea of directly elected town mayors, managers or chief executives. I doubt if that is the right structure but that might be better decided after having distinguished between the broad categories of services in a way described above.

Proposals for elected regional authorites are clearly undesirable. There would be little for them to do unless they grabbed powers best exercised locally by councils or those best exercised nationally, and to be effective they would need powers of independent powers of taxation too. The latter is particularly unacceptable. Parliament fought for centuries to achieve the sole power to tax. It should franchise such powers only with the greatest reluctance and caution, never granting them by right to any other authority.

At its heart that is the argument against devolution – a system which could only undermine the integrity of the Union. Where more widespread powers are needed, independent bodies appointed by Government (quangos) such as the National Rivers Authority are the most effective instruments and it may well be that the fire service would benefit from a similar reform.

That the Union should be upheld is an imperative of government, and talk of devolution in Ulster undermines both its status as a part of the Kingdom akin to all other regions and the stand against devolution in Scotland and Wales. If terrorism is to be defeated in Ulster and prevented from arising in Scotland and Wales it must be seen to have gained no concessions whatsoever from the Government. Almost as important there must be no doubts about the permanence of the Union and it is therefore essential that the shape of the government of Ulster must be no different to that of England, Scotland or Wales.

I view the creation of a Conservative Party in Ulster with considerable misgivings but if it has any purpose at all it should be to campaign that Ulster should be governed no differently to the remainder of the Kingdom. Anything which makes Ulster different makes it vulnerable, and if Ulster's place in the Kingdom is undermined so too will be those of Scotland and Wales. It is worth bearing in mind in the context of Europe too the importance of language in maintaining or destroying the consent of people to share a common government. Welsh nationalism has had little appeal to the Welsh, and Welsh- and English-born people have lived harmoniously together for many years, but the aggressive promotion of the Welsh language as a means of dividing communities against each other illustrates the role of language in the creation of national consciousness.

As I have implied elsewhere in this book, the most powerful force for change in our constitution and system of government is the European Community. It is a force generated from outside our shores and, by overwhelming majority, by people not of our nationality. That is to say, it is a foreign force. It is far from being the first time that we have been influenced by foreigners or by ideas generated abroad but it is a very long time since we last suffered from laws made outside our shores by foreigners, required to be enforced by our judicial system.

Until recently the impact of the laws has been generally acceptable. This is not least because although made by a foreign institution they have been given effect by our own legislation, legislation which could be revoked by Parliament which retains sovereignty in the name of the Monarch. Such a revocation would be a tumultuous affair with far-reaching consequences, but it is both technically and practically possible. We are bound by the Treaty of Rome but treaties can be renounced and revoked by sovereign nations. What is now in prospect is the progressive derogation of sovereignty – that is, the right of self-government to the stage at which it might be neither technically nor practically within the power of Parliament to reverse the process of change from independent self-governing nation to province. The return to independence and self-government could then be achieved only by either an act of the governing state, that is the sovereign authority of the European community, or by rebellion against that authority.

It is devoutly to be hoped that such a situation will never arise – and it is certain in my mind that the British will not accept extinction of their right to independent self-governing nationhood any more than have the Latvians, Lithuanians, Estonians, Serbs, Croats, Slovenes, Czechs, Greek Cypriots, Turkish Cypriots and many others. Indeed the history of attempts to weld into single states linguistically separate communities is not encouraging, a fact well illustrated by the current moves to split Belgium into two virtually independent entities on linguistic lines. Almost the only example of such success has been that of the United States, where it was achieved (the slaves apart) by immigration into a vastly under-populated land by immigrants required to and prepared to accept its existing constitution, law and practice and above all the language of its founders. Until recently such immigrants were also largely cut off from their lands of origin by distance and the costs of travel as well as the despotic regimes from which many had fled. Ethnic politics has nonetheless always been a potentially disruptive force wherever ethnic minorities concentrated to form electoral blocs. Sadly, as modern technology has brought long-distance travel to the masses a lack of national will has begun to undermine the single-language policy and encourage ethnic politics which may put under threat the integrity of even the United States.

The importance of language is not just that it reflects past and guides future cultural patterns. A democratic state must have a sense of national identity and of national public opinion to sustain it. Without a common language it is almost imposs-ible for either to exist.

The clash between British and continental attitudes springs from the differences of history, law, language and culture. There is perhaps nothing inherently right or wrong about our island way or the continental way and it is clearly easy enough for individual Britons to live happily enough in France, Italy or elsewhere. They are not, however, French, nor Italian and in general they neither commit themselves to be so, nor deny themselves the right to return home to their full citizenship. Equally many continentals find life in Britain tolerable enough to stay for many years, without loss of nationality.

Those differences of attitude make it possible for nationals of our European partners to look with an equanimity we cannot share at a prospective loss of statehood. It is not, however, a British objection to continental ways which is the sticking point. Even if a Euro super-state were to be constructed by the extension of the Westminster political system, British law, the

Monarchy and the whole apparatus of state, it would still not be acceptable. The key issue is self-government, the right to manage our own affairs, the unilateral right of the people of this kingdom not only to change their government and thereby its policies but even to change step by step the very constitution.

At what point would movement towards monetary, economic and political union rob the citizens of member states of the ability to determine their own affairs? To a considerable extent that right has been fretted away by the extension of the Community competence and by majority voting in the Council of Ministers. No doubt Sir Geoffrey Howe was saying what he believed to be true when he told the House of Commons that the Single European Act would leave member states able to insist on unanimity on matters of vital interest – the Luxembourg Compromise. In practice that veto has become subject to the majority view of what is or is not a vital interest and is therefore of diminishing use. However, we – like other signatories of the Treaty of Rome – remain sovereign states and therefore have the undoubted right to renounce the Treaty. Since that is our only defence against the imposition of policies which are against our interest, it is time that a proper assessment was made of the impact of renunciation. Alongside that study, policies to minimise the disadvantage and maximise the advantage of life outside the Community should be developed. Clearly since our trade with our partners is in deficit they would no more wish to erect barriers than would we. We would be able to open our domestic markets to imports of food at prices which would have a significant effect on inflation, as well as to reform our system of agricultural support, so the balance of advantage and disadvantage would be far from all one-way.

Our aim should be to stay within the Community – but at present we negotiate as though that was not only the aim but the only possible course for us. That is a poor base from which to develop policy and a weak position from which to negotiate.

It is also time we assessed how far we are willing to go along the path of monetary, economic and political union leading to a single state as outlined by M. Delors, Herr Kohl and others.

There can be no doubt about the ambition of Herr Kohl to form a European super-state, and we would be wise to accept that he meant what he said on 13 March 1991 in the Bundestag.

> Our primary objective all along has been the political unification of Europe. We need a united and strong Europe ... The Federal Government will therefore make every effort to achieve European union before the next election for the European Parliament in the spring of 1994 ... We would like the European Parliament to have far greater powers ... A common foreign and security policy must be developed which in the longer term will also embrace common European defence ... However important the completion of economic and monetary union it would remain mere patchwork unless political union were established simultaneously. These two undertakings are, in our opinion, inseparable.

It seems clear to me that one sticking point for Britain will be the creation of a single currency. A common currency is acceptable since although it would share advantages and disadvantages with a single currency it would not have the character of near irrevocability. Our national finances would continue to be conducted in sterling, a currency managed by wholly British institutions under British law, which could be devalued or revalued against the common currency if that seemed desirable. There is no guarantee that the common currency would be better managed than sterling, or for that matter than the mark, lira, peseta or franc. It might come to be regarded as 'paper gold' – or it might not. Sterling might, or might not, remain stable against it, but it would remain a separate currency.

To suggest, as Commissioner Leon Brittan has done, that British reservations about a single currency are mere sentimentality about sterling which could be dealt with by printing ECU notes with a sterling equivalent on the reverse side, is either infantile or calculated to mislead. One might as well suggest that Wales and Ulster would regain separate monetary sovereignty if sterling notes were printed with leeks, or the Red Hand, on their backs. Even more to the point it is clear that the issue of Scottish sterling notes today does not imply the existence of separate Scottish monetary policies nor of a separate Chancellor of the Exchequer of Scotland.

If there is to be drawn a line in the sand over which the United Kingdom could not pass without setting out along the path to the status of a province, not nation, it is the creation of a single currency. From that moment on, the British Chancellor of the Exchequer's economic powers would be comparable to those of the treasurer of a permanently rate- or charge-capped local authority – or perhaps more accurately they would be akin to those of the Secretaries of State for Scotland, Wales or Northern Ireland.

After the annexation of East Germany by West Germany and the imposition of a single currency throughout the new greater Germany, there can be no doubt of the importance of such a step. Herr Pöhl, as head of the supposedly independent Bundesbank, complained bitterly that the imposition was carried out at the wrong exchange rate between East and West marks, and subsequently announced his resignation. So much for the hopes of those who pine for an independent Euro-Bank to manage the single currency! The Bundesbank was never truly independent, it was merely that for many years Germany enjoyed politicians wise enough not to override the wishes of the bank, and sometimes sufficiently cynical to pretend that unpopular policies which they wanted to impose were the work of the bank, not themselves.

The soaring unemployment in East Germany and the widening economic gap between East and West Germans are the practical effects of the use of a single currency within a single economic system with substantial disparities or divergences. The resentment of West Germans being faced with the bills to buy off the resentment of East Germans whose previously lower standard of living is sinking even lower, is a political effect of the single currency. There is a similar effect in Italy where for more than 100 years the use of a single currency has widened and reinforced the economic divergence between the prosperous North based in Turin and the poor South based in Naples.

At this point, however, I am concerned not to show how a single currency would be a political and economic disaster for the European Community but with the constitutional effects upon the United Kingdom and to suggest a way out of the Community's dilemma. Not only politicians, but Herr Pöhl have pointed out that some Community member states are ready now to move towards monetary, economic and political union. This, so it is held, leaves the United Kingdom a choice only between joining now or being 'left behind', having no voice in the planning of the new European Community structure, yet being compelled eventually to join and fit in as best we may. The only way to protect our interest, it is argued, is to operate tactically, postponing the crunch decisions for as long as possible and, like East Germany, 'getting the best terms possible' for our eventual absorption into the super state.

There is, however, a different approach. The Treaty of Rome, is working satisfactorily and needs no further major changes. Those member states anxious to proceed to closer union are free to do so along the lines of the union of England, Scotland, Ulster and Wales. Within the United Kingdom we have achieved all the objectives of the most ambitious European unionists. After some centuries of experience we understand the problems, the mechanisms, the implications and both the advantages and disadvantages. When the United Kingdom entered the European Community all four peoples of the Union entered together. There is no reason at all why those member states who wish should not follow the example of the English, Scots, Welsh and Northern Irish and form a United Kingdom or Republic of their own. French, German, Italians, Luxemburgers, perhaps Dutch and either Flemings or Walloons or both, could decide to elect their representatives to a single governing assembly of what we might call the West-Central European Republic. They would enjoy common taxation, common laws and obligations, common foreign and defence policies and armed forces, common social security systems, in fact monetary, economic and political union.

The old nation states would fall away, their national parliaments would be dissolved (their Members being redundant) and the West-Central Republic would become a member of the European Community alongside the United Kingdom, Spain, Portugal, the Republic of Ireland and Greece.

The advantages of a progressive union of this kind are clear. First of all it would not affect the states of those nations wishing to preserve their rights to self-government including independent monetary and legal authorities, defence and foreign policies. Second, the new Republic would be a showcase for European union allowing the more cautious states the opportunity to be convinced that nationalism is indeed dead and that neither French, Dutch, Flemings, Walloon, Germans or Italians are unwilling to concede making over their national affairs to others. Third, it would allow other states, Norway, Sweden, Switzerland, Austria, Hungary, Czechoslovakia, Poland and more to start more easily on the path to full membership of the Community.

In short we could all both have our cake and eat it, however bitter or sweet it might be.

Better by far that the West-Central European Republic ended in tears and recriminations than that the whole Community and every member state should do so.

It should be a prime objection of British policy to achieve the enlargement, not the break-up of the European Community. The preservation of the ancient rights of the British people to their own constitution and to self-government is not an impediment but a prerequisite to the success of that policy.

CHAPTER FIVE

The Creation of Wealth

The three Thatcher administrations of 1979, 1983 and 1987–1990 rescued the United Kingdom from its slide towards the public, private and political squalor and poverty of socialism. None the less there are still serious problems which remain to be tackled.

On the economic front whilst trades union reform, deregulation, lower and more stable corporate taxation have all benefitted industry and commerce, the rebuilding of manufacturing industry has proved a slow and frustrating exercise. Institutional investors have long memories but limited vision. Although they have been ready to finance projects requiring heavy front-end loading and long pay-back periods as in aerospace or even the Channel Tunnel, they have been equally ready to favour takeover bids for companies whose short-term profitability might be enhanced by cutting back on long-term investment – a factor which has probably influenced many manufacturing companies to avoid the risk of takeover by limiting their own spending on long-term projects.

Following the prosecution in the USA of Mr Milliken and

Drexel Burnham Lambert, the American merchant banking house, and more recently in 1990 the rash of junk bond failures, the financing of speculative takeover bids and buyouts by junk bonds has become markedly less fashionable. It may well be that the alleged 'short-termism' of institutional investors (which has in my view been exaggerated) will have less influence in future since the current depression of companies' share prices also makes speculative bids financed by paper less likely.

However, it cannot be denied that for smaller public companies a combination of the risk of aggressive takeover and the difficulty of achieving the scale required to compete with major established foreign businesses in Britain's very open markets make it unlikely that new indigenous companies will be successfully established in industries such as motor manufacturing. By 1979 a combination of high inflation, erratic economic regulation, ill-advised government-inspired takeovers and mergers, and poorly judged private ones too, atrocious industrial relations, and prices and income policies had all but wiped out large sectors of manufacturing industry, the indigenous motor manufacturers amongst them. In the early eighties a low point was reached when a final closure of the state-owned British Leyland (subsequently Rover Group) was not ruled out and there was a real possibility of progressive withdrawal by Ford and General Motors. The Japanese connection, first through the Honda–British Leyland alliance, then the establishment of manufacturing by Nissan and later by Toyota, increased investment by Peugeot–Citroën, Ford and General Motors, and Rover Group's return to the private sector and profitability have re-established motor manufacturing on a scale which will have a significant impact in the mid-1990s. Quite remarkably, during the 1990/91 recession car output rose in the UK with exports growing sharply – a clear contrast with the experience of earlier years.

Such success is encouraging, as is the remarkable progress

since denationalisation of Rolls-Royce, the only world-class aero-engine manufacturer outside the United States, British Aerospace, the leading non-American company in its field, and British Steel. These are world-class manufacturing companies standing alongside ICI and GEC, but no country as small as the United Kingdom could conceivably be home to more than a handful of such businesses. We also have some of the world's leading service businesses – British Airways, British Telecom, P & O and the like – as well as a leading financial services sector. It is clear, however, that there are wide gaps in manufacturing industry. Much has been made by the Government's critics of the lack of a major British manufacturer of data-processing machines but a more sober assessment suggests that in the Europe of 1992 and within a progressively more open world trading system such a lack is not a critical factor. Of far greater importance is the ability to obtain and use effectively such equipment, which is well demonstrated by service companies such as British Telecom (one of the world's leading three or four companies in its field) and those within the financial sector.

As in the motor industry, foreign investment in other sectors, notably that of Japan, has plugged some gaps. For example the United Kingdom is now a net exporter of colour television receivers, but a marked overall lack of home production of domestic electrical appliances of many kinds still persists.

Unhelpful taxation policies, erratic economic management and unstable industrial relations have been particularly harmful to the growth of independently or privately owned businesses. Germany tends to be rich in such enterprises but here in Britain we have all too few such companies. JCB, the family-owned business whose name is formed from the initials of the founder, Joe Bamford, is remarkable in Britain for its size and success; yet in Germany it would not be unusual. Its success is such that JCB has become a generic name for all back hoe loader-excavators across the free world. However, few such family businesses in Britain have become strong enough to achieve world status. Sooner or later either their growth or independence is prejudiced by the incidence of death duties, inheritance tax or discriminatory tax on investment income, forcing a choice between capital starvation or the disposal of shares and loss of family control.

The significance of these deficiencies should not be exaggerated. Although the heavy trade deficit in manufactured goods is currently too great to be overcome by the surplus on oil and invisibles, the trends are almost all in the right direction but too slow and too open to reversal during periods of economic growth. International crises apart, such reverses are most likely to arise from economic mismanagement – primarily monetary mismanagement leading to high inflation and consequently high interest rates. Currently there is a belief, most widely spread amongst those who have in the past believed in many magic solutions to our problems, that the ERM, the Euro-Fed or a single currency would miraculously end such difficulties. Such hopes are likely to be dashed – as were those built on nationalisation, central planning, tripartitism, EDC, NEDCs, incomes policies and social contracts, and other soft-option magic remedies.

In contrast the Government's industrial policies have been generally right and mostly successful. The disengagement of Government – that is of politicians and officials – from the business of business has been beneficial. Investment and management decisions are no longer tailored to the prevailing (usually short-term) political nostrums of the day. With no cushion of tax-financed bail-outs to fall back upon, the temptation to delay difficult management decisions is sharply lessened and technical and financial controls in business have greatly improved during the 1990s. The changes in regional policy which sharply reduced the subsidies available to industry in the so-called less developed areas were widely criticised but in contrast to earlier recessions the economic slowdown of 1990 bit earlier and more deeply in the overheated South than in the regions with spare capacity. In short, there is increasingly strong evidence that a major factor in the inability of the northern regions to regenerate independent and healthy economic activity was the industrial subsidy system inherent in the regional policies followed by successive governments from 1945 to 1980. However, the subsidy to facilitate the clean-up of industrial areas which had fallen into disuse, leaving market forces to bring in new enterprises, has proved to be an effective use of taxpayers' money. Such subsidy is non-discriminatory between one business and another and does not require officials or politicians to make business decisions. Sadly there has also had to be a limited use of mainly discriminatory subsidy to counter those offered by other European Community countries to attract inward investment.

Improvements to transport infrastructures have also played a significant part in improving the attractiveness of areas more distant from the major consumer markets. But the major attractions for industry have proved to be accommodation costs far lower than in the more prosperous areas and a better availability of labour. One failure of the Thatcher years has been the extent to which the cost of labour has remained obstinately unrelated to its supply because of rigid national pay bargaining by reactionary unions. Fortunately a degree of competition between unions has begun to undermine that rigidity and, in the less unionised service sector and amongst female labour, lower costs have proved an effective antidote to unemployment and a successful regional policy. Lower labour costs do not necessarily mean a lower standard of living for the workers concerned, as they may well be financed by higher productivity as less restrictive practices encourage higher investment in new technology rather than reliance upon lower wages to reduce costs. Even where take-home pay is lower than in the South East the workers, like their employers, benefit from the lower costs of accommodation and the lower costs of travel to work too.

What more remains then to be done? Where are the weaknesses in our system which are open to be corrected by Government action?

One of the largest factors has been the high propensity of British people to spend out of current earned income rather than to save and invest to enjoy investment income – that is personal as opposed to institutional short-termism – and the gross distortion caused by the subsidy of investment in owner-occupied accommodation as opposed to wealth-creating business activity.

Norman Lamont's first budget bravely took the first step towards abolition of mortgage interest tax relief. There is little doubt that the Treasury accepts that whilst the tax subsidy of borrowing for house purchase by owner occupiers has been well justified by the growth in home ownership, which is socially and economically more desirable than large-scale municipal landlordism, it is now outliving its usefulness. Partly under its influence, house prices had inflated to the extent that many purchasers benefit to the full extent of the interest on a £30,000 loan at the 40 per cent rate, that is £1,200 at a mortgage rate of 10% or £1,800 at 15% per annum. The sums involved had become huge with a theoretical total of £7.8 billion annual revenue forgone. That consequential enhanced purchasing power for housing has been a major factor in the inflation of house prices, which in turn has been a major factor in financing a growth in personal spending and indebtedness. In turn that then added pressure in pay bargaining which has needlessly pushed up output prices. Unless such price rises are accommodated by monetary growth (that is by inflation), unemployment is the first consequence. If it is so accommodated then inflation comes first and unemployment follows later.

A modest decline in the amount of purchasing power available for house purchase, particularly if it was seen to be a long-term trend and not a part of a short-term cycle, would not affect the rate of building since it is not building costs but land prices which have inflated to drive up house prices. The benign effect of a gentle decline in house and land prices in real terms would also extend to the rented sector in which economic rents are inordinately high. The subsidies paid to less well-off tenants are a subsidy to land prices and the owners of building land rather than to the poor.

At present the business of letting residential accommodation is no more truly profitable than is agriculture since neither can show a satisfactory yield on capital employed unless account is taken of future growth in the price of houses (by which we mean building land) or of agricultural land arising out of inflation, scarcity, subsidy and the prospect of planning consent for development.

Had Nigel Lawson's 1988 Budget limited tax relief on mortage interest to the standard 25 per cent income-tax rate rather than allowing the relief to be used at the 40 per cent rate by higher-rate payers, the 1988/89 house price boom would have been at least abated. The public's acceptance of this change in Norman Lamont's 1991 Budget shows that such a change would have been quite acceptable within the context of Mr Lawson's Budget which brought such substantial benefits to higher-rate taxpayers in particular. It is only fair to say that I believe Nigel Lawson would have wanted to make the change himself but Mrs Thatcher was convinced that it would be damaging to the Government.

Both the direct effect of such a change and the signal it gives that the days of easy, substantial real increases in house prices have come to an end should have a profound effect upon patterns of spending and saving. Unfortunately its impact was undermined by an apparent assurance that the process would go no further than the ending of the 40 per cent rate of relief.

If the fear (or hope) that house prices would inevitably escalate faster than the R P I was removed, younger people might well be less anxious to enter the market as purchasers and prefer instead to save whilst renting a home or at least to buy an easily affordable house rather than striving for the most expensive they could possibly finance. New savings generated would then be far more likely to find their way either directly or indirectly through institutions such as banks and insurance companies into the financing of industry and commerce, inducing a pressure towards lower rather than higher interest rates.

In the 1991 Budget higher-rate taxpayers were broadly compensated for the lessening of tax relief on their mortgages by an increase in the threshold of the 40 per cent rate. It is likely that future erosion of the relief will come naturally through the reduction of the standard 25 per cent rate towards 20 per cent. By that means the concession which on a 10 per cent fixed-rate mortgage before 1988 was worth as much as £1,800 (set against the then 60 per cent rate), in 1990 up to £1,200, and in 1991 £750, would with tax at 20 per cent be reduced in value to £600.

However, if savings and investing as opposed to borrowing is really to be encouraged, then some of the revenue no longer forgone on mortgage interest tax relief might be used to encourage savers. PEPs and TESSAs are undoubtedly useful but they are distortions of the tax system, and a broader and less discriminatory approach is needed. That could well involve a substantial increase in the level of capital gains exemption which should be widened to accommodate investment income as well. If the unused portion of that exemption could be rolled up for a period of twenty years at least, to be set against liability to inheritance tax, it would also mitigate the problems caused by that tax to the building up of strong well-financed family businesses.

A further difficulty for industry has arisen from competition policy, which has at times been confused and capricious. Sometimes quite irrelevant considerations such as regional political susceptibilities have influenced policy. At other times policy has seemed unduly moved by a quixotic view favouring an idealised market comprising a multiplicity of small suppliers. Whilst in some sectors that is achievable and desirable, in others it is neither. For example, within the limitations of the post-war commitment to a mixed economy it was important to uphold the place of private enterprise airlines to offer innovative services (the package-tour holiday concept and cheap charter flights began in that way). But once British Airways had been denationalised and international competition became strengthened by deregulation, it was not competition between British carriers but international competition which governed the market. It became progressively more unrealistic to seek to maintain two British flag carriers but the Government still harboured the romantic notion of competition between British Caledonian and British Airways, with the successful major carrier being cut down in size to benefit the struggling B-Cal. Such hostility to the big and successful was narrowly overcome at that time. British Airways was almost prevented from counterbidding when the foreign carrier SAS sought to take over the ailing B-Cal in order to achieve a competitive position simply not open to a British carrier in foreign markets. More recently in March 1991 Transport Secretary Rifkind refused to heed the lessons of the collapse of so many British airlines which had been promoted as the competitive spur to British Airways. Eagle, Laker, B-Cal, Air Europe had all followed similar sad histories. Only British Midland, so far determined not to over-expand, has offered any encouragement to the multi-flag-carrier policy, yet Mr Rifkind aggressively attacked British Airways and has promoted Virgin Airlines as the latest British challenger, seemingly oblivious to the lessons of the past. Even worse he has given American carriers advantages in the British market without any compensatory advantages for British Airways in the American market. One can only wonder for how long this time British Airways will be weakened before the sad lesson is learned once again.

A similar hostility has been shown towards British Telecommunications plc. Whilst both British Airways and BT are threatened with competition at home from large foreign rivals operating from entirely protected home markets, the British Government seems still to hanker after the break-up of such dominant business in the hope of more vigorous competition in the British market. Fortunately in the 1991 review of competition in the telecommunications industry BT's arguments were so powerful that the worst excesses of this naïve policy were avoided. But there is no doubt that it remains a dream amongst regulators and some officials and Ministers. Competition there would certainly be, as the British mini airlines and telephone businesses were devoured or destroyed by larger and stronger foreign competitors who would soon be large enough to challenge the formerly powerful British firms in the home market and destroy them overseas. There is no doubt that competition is highly desirable in air transport and telecommunications and it is quite possible to ensure it in most market sectors, but it should be lasting competition on a fair basis and not predicated on the assumption that size is of itself sinful in British (but not foreign) businesses operating in industries which already, or will soon, compete on a global scale.

Much has been made of the problems caused to British industry by the very wide fluctuations in the parity of sterling against such key currencies as the US dollar and the Deutschmark. There can be no doubt that life would be easier if one variable at least was removed from those likely to undermine business plans. However, there is not too much agreement on what rate business would like for sterling, nor indeed sufficient understanding that a currency is worth not what its originators would like it to be worth but what the world is willing to pay for it. Fixing sterling against the D-Mark, for example, still leaves it floating alongside the Mark against the dollar and the yen, and fixing also brings costs of its own. There can be no doubt that Mr Lawson's elongated inflationary blip (the underlying cause of the fall of Mrs Thatcher) sprang from his policy of 'shadowing' the D-Mark at a time when sterling was rising strongly. In his efforts to hold sterling down, interest rates were cut and cut again giving an excessive boost to our already ebullient economy. The effect of the 1988 Budget tax cuts was in itself quite small, not least since those arose in the context of a negative PSBR or a surplus of some £14.5 billion – surely a take-away, not a give-away budget. More recently, following entry to the ERM, domestic policy was constrained by the need to keep sterling from falling below its lower limit. Interest rates therefore remained high at a time when many monetarists, looking at the monetary aggregates, most particularly Mo, would have been calling for cheaper money to avoid an excessively deep recession or even a slump.

I am not entirely convinced by that view since in the first quarter of 1991 the underlying rate of UK inflation remained high, with only a limited fall in immediate prospect before the third quarter. However, there can be no doubt that UK economic policy became more directly tied to the needs of the German economy than need be. This uncomfortable fact is overlooked by the enthusiasts for fixed exchange rates in their own right and by their current fellow travellers, the Euro-fanatics, for whom membership of the ERM is a political necessity whose economic effects are bound to be benign because 'being in Europe' is a good thing. That is at best an untried assertion which rests upon two dubious assumptions. First, that what is good for the German economy is good for ours and that the two economic cycles are bound to be in step, and, second, that German economic management will always be better than British economic management.

The growing problem in Germany arising from reunification may well weaken the Mark to the extent that sterling will bump against the top of its parity band. No doubt there would then be pressure both from British exporters and the German authorities for British interest rates to be lowered more quickly than is prudent. In that case I hope that the Germans are firmly told it is a problem of their economy and they should raise their rates.

Twenty years ago German economic superiority was manifested by the appalling industrial relations problems in Britain contrasted with the harmony perceived in Germany. We were frequently told that to achieve a German standard of days lost in industrial disputes we would have to adopt German-style co-determination and two-tier company boards. Seminars on the subject ran almost without a break, becoming a growth industry in their own right. Little is now heard of this matter. More recently the erstwhile experts on industrial relations have become experts on inflation, pointing out that the German record in this field is greatly superior to that of the United Kingdom. This view would not be shared by my father's generation, most of whom died before our great inflation (a peak of some 30 per cent in a year) but remembered quite clearly German inflation at several thousand per cent. In fact Britain's long-term record is best illustrated by the fact that until our coinage was decimalised in the early 1970s, old pennies (of which there were 240 to the £) and half pennies minted more than one hundred years earlier were still in use. There can be few of our Community partners who could make a similar claim.

Just as our industrial relations policies had all but eliminated the British disease of incessant strikes, Thatcherite policies had all but eliminated the German advantage on inflation until the unfortunate experiment in shadowing the Mark led to the famous Lawson blip of almost 11 per cent year on year. It would therefore be unwise to suppose that success in this field can come only by tying ourselves to the wheels of the German economy just as it was proven to be unwise to suppose that the German route was the only route to better industrial relations.

It must surely be that in the medium, let alone long term, the value of a currency is set by the strength of its national economy relative to other economies rather than that an economy can be made weak or strong by a political decision to fix the parity of the currency at a particular level. Currencies will remain stable relative to each other only if their economies remain stable relative to each other. So whilst stability or gentle change is an ideal to be sought, it can be achieved only as a result of other economic policies and it should not be an over-riding policy objective to be pursued at the expense of more substantial matters.

Another frequently cited cause of our relatively poor economic performance is a lack of training in Britain. No doubt there is something in this but it is grossly overstated.

In the late nineteenth and early twentieth centuries the British apprentice training scheme was well ahead of those of other countries. The tragedy was that because of the mis-conceived self-interest of monopolistic unions it remained unre-formed, until by the 1980s it had become almost incapable of being reformed and entered rapid decline. Today it has been widely abandoned in industry and now maintains its nine-teenth-century standing only in the profession of barrister at law. It is the more difficult to compare our training standards with those practised abroad because of a lack of appropriate agreed definitions, practices or terms. The payment of training subsidies or imposition of levies in some countries further obscures the picture. Certainly where training is subsidised or where employers failing to spend up to arbitrary benchmarks are forced to pay a training levy, reported expenditure on training rises rapidly. No doubt if we adopted (or re-adopted) such systems, reported spending on training would rapidly increase. Whether any more training would be done is a different matter.

In my own time as Secretary of State for Employment I failed to achieve the agreement of most trades unions to modernise apprentice training. Where unions did accept the need for change, most notably the EEPTU, the apprentice system has survived and prospered. Elsewhere new systems and new qualifications have been devised, particularly during the tenure of office of Norman Fowler. Much remains to be done, particularly in tidying up the wide assortment of qualifications and examinations. Most training will inevitably be given by employers and being specific to the job of the particular employee concerned will not be as freely transferable or marketable as it should be. Employees should therefore be encouraged to seek formal qualifications based on their in-work training and, although much has been achieved, even more still needs to be done.

However, it is highly encouraging that for all the claimed differences between the industrial training policies of the Government and the Labour Party the structures now being established are not in great dispute. Even if there was a change of government it is unlikely there would be a great upheaval or reversal of policy and it may well be that after a very difficult period industrial training is entering a calmer and more constructive phase. It is sad that the old system could not be reformed and updated, and much to be hoped that the greater flexibility and acceptance of the new will enable the skills shortage and training gap with our competitors to be overcome.

Important as training is, education is far more so. It is the basis from which skills can be acquired and it shapes the attitudes of each generation of workers.

The reform of education is dealt with in Chapter 6 but it is clear that however successful it may be, a centrally directed system is bound, sooner or later, to go awry on a large scale, whilst a market-based system will naturally correct its own errors and failings incrementaly.

All experience demonstrates that governments, whether democratic or authoritarian, are poorly equipped to own or manage commercial enterprises. Of course examples of success can be found, but they are few in relation to those of failure, whereas in the market system the reverse is true. All too often discussion around such a statement centres upon the survival or collapse of individual enterprises. Not surprisingly, in such a context the survival rate of state or state-protected enterprises is likely to be better than private-sector businesses in a vigorous market economy. That, however, is not the appropriate criterion. The test is not the survival of particular enterprises but the success of the system in supplying the goods and services demanded by its consumers. Frequently the very existence of state businesses prevents – by use of monopolistic market domination and subsidy paid for by its competitors or regulation – the creation of new businesses which would provide better, cheaper or more appropriate goods or services.

It is clear therefore that our future industrial and commercial success, which is itself an absolute condition of success in most other fields, requires a continuing programme of privatization of the remaining state-owned commercial activities. There is room for argument as to whether trunk roads or railways can sensibly be privatized or not. It may well be that almost all trunk roads and motorways are, because of the difficulty of arranging any form of competition, best left as they are, publicly owned, built and maintained by competitive contract. Railways offer a better prospect although it may well be neither possible nor desirable to privatise both the permanent way and the operation of train services, but certainly the present overall state-owned and badly run monopoly must be privatised so far as is practicable and properly managed and regulated where it is not.

A government free from ownership is freed from the conflict of interest inevitably posed with regulation and whilst ownership is not the business of the state, regulation directly or by approved agencies certainly is.

In my experience the present main regulatory system, that of the Office of Fair Trading, the Monopolies and Mergers Commission and the Department of Trade and Industry works well, provided the Director General of OFT, the Chairman of the MMC and the Secretary of State are themselves effective personalities with comparable views on policy. All three bodies need shake-ups and changes of leadership from time to time, although it might well be argued that they have been much too frequent at DTI and too infrequent at MMC. Competition policy needs to be simple, well designed, clearly understood, predictable and, where references are made to the OFT or MMC, the outcome should not be unduly delayed. The principal threat to the system is now the ambition of the EC Commission to take control and achieve for industry what it has done for agriculture.

On the whole the making of enquiries by Inspectors appointed by the Secretary of State has worked well. But having both commissioned enquiries, setting terms of reference and appointing Inspectors and been called upon to give evidence before two enquiries, I believe that in one respect at least practice could be improved. In general the calibre of Inspectors has been impressive and there is no doubt in my mind that the forensic qualities and independence of professional lawyers are particularly well suited to the taking, sifting and assessment of evidence. The appointment of senior counsel also has the advantage that the nature of that profession leads to the availability of first-class people able to devote themselves almost full-time if needs be for the duration of an enquiry. However, although the need of expert additional knowledge is often acknowledged by the appointment of accountants to sit along-side counsel, it is rare for the need of similarly expert advice on business and commercial practice to be accepted. It would be difficult to find working company directors who could leave their executive duties to sit through a substantial enquiry. But I believe it would be helpful if recently retired experienced directors were to be appointed where appropriate, either as Inspectors or as advisors or assessors to assist counsel who should remain the mainstay of DTI enquiries.

Regrettably, in recent years, the entirely proper and much needed disengagement from the management, ownership and direction of industry and commerce has led to a belief, not totally without foundation, that the Government felt that its political, ideological, regulatory and monetary rectitude, parity and independence would be threatened by any form of contact with businesses employing more than 200 people. In my opinion government needs to understand the problems and needs of industry and cannot properly fulfil its obligation to create a climate favourable to wealth creation unless it is prop-erly informed about commercial matters. Both government and industry would have benefited at times from a better under-standing of each other's policies than is likely to be achieved either by the CBI turning up at the governing party's annual conference or Ministers visiting the CBI conference in turn. That is not to call for the DTI to become as dominated by businessmen as is the Department of Health by the medical profession, the Ministry of Agriculture by landowning and farming interests, the Department of Education by edu-cationalists or the Foreign Office by foreigners. It is to call for a sensible, well-informed but not cosy relationship between commerce and industry and government.

Much is made of the alleged need for government to subsidise or in some way to influence the research and development programmes and the capital investment of industry. There is little chance of such initiatives bearing fruit. The best assurance of fruitful investment, whether in research and development or in plant and machinery, training and product improvement, is that the end-products will be sold profitably and the profits so generated will be taxed at the lowest possible rate. That assurance has already been given in part since business now enjoys corporate taxation lower in Britain than in almost anywhere amongst our competitors. However, we have suffered both inflation and interest rates higher and more volatile than in many other economies. Subject only to the risk of a change of government those volatilities and unfavourable comparisons should be coming to an end in the early 1990s.

There will continue to be a role for government-sponsored research, and hopefully industry will feel able to take more advantage of it than in the past when the result of much research financed by British taxpayers was developed into products manufactured by Japanese and German companies. There is also still more to be done to help companies harvest profits from their investment in research through better protection of intellectual property. Sadly at times the Government has seemed more interested in the short-term popularity amongst consumers when the protection given to intellectual property is weakened, than by the long-term benefits when research and development are encouraged and financed by the profits gained from the exploitation of intellectual property by its owners.

The reforms of personal taxation described earlier and those in education and training are vital to our economic success. Perhaps above all we still need to see stronger signals from government and the establishment more widely that success in industry and commerce is esteemed at least as highly as success in sport, the media, government or the arts and entertainment –

and perhaps even more than success in the lottery of the choice of one's parents.

It is to be hoped that might be achieved in John Major's 'classless' society. It is certainly not to be expected from the mean, envious, spiteful and splenetic half-baked socialism of the intellectually rootless leadership of the Labour Party.

CHAPTER SIX

Proposals for Change

My approach to political problem-solving has always been based on the assumption that the great majority of people normally act as individuals in a logically comprehensible manner. In a society in which the structure of financial, moral and social incentives and disincentives is benign then on the whole individuals will respond in socially and economically beneficial ways. Similarly when the system of penalties, rewards, risks and opportunities is perversely constructed then the outcome will normally be perverse or anti-social.

Perhaps one of the most obvious recent examples of this effect in Britain is the conduct of industrial relations during the post-war period. The commitment of successive governments to full employment and a universal benefit system, combined with industrial relations law under which trades unions were immune from actions in tort, together with trades union law permitting a lack of proper democratic procedures within unions, led inevitably to large-scale misuse and under-utilisation of labour. This was accompanied by low wages alongside high labour costs and an appallingly high level of industrial disputes and stoppages. To complete the perverse structure, trades unions could (and still can) buy votes to be cast in the election of Labour Party leaders, the making of that Party's policies at its Conference and the nomination of parliamentary candidates, by affiliating their members to that Party. In practice such affiliation requires neither the consent nor even knowledge of the member concerned and the numbers affiliated by a union could, and have, exceeded its total membership. Nor do individual members have much say in how the block votes (blocks of over a million in some cases) are cast. With such powerful political patronage at the command of leaders, some of whom held office for life once elected in blatantly crooked ballots, it is hardly surprising that the partisan political interests of the leaders frequently overrode the legitimate interests of the members. What is more, Labour Governments had neither the will nor the power to reform the corrupt system.

The wide political consensus – 'Butskellism' – of the 1960s and the intellectual climate of state intervention in industrial disputes (which had been strengthened by the wartime practice of centralised economic planning) led to major industrial disputes, even those entirely within the private sector, frequently being settled through government intervention. The 'beer and sandwiches' routine was widely practised at successive levels: shop-floor, company, trade association, ACAS (the state-sponsored Advisory, Conciliation and Arbitration Service), official and ministerial levels at the Department of Labour or Employment, and finally 10 Downing Street. Major trades union leaders (acting quite logically within the perverse framework) ensured that gains were made at each bargaining level before finally arriving to be photographed and televised giving impromptu press conferences on the doorstep of Number 10. Not unnaturally the general public perceived such men to be immensely powerful and important, rating in one public opinion poll the leader of the transport workers' union to be more powerful than the Prime Minister of the day.

Mr Heath's brave attempt to reform trades union and industrial law failed because it left in place the system of legal immunities and together with his state control of pay and prices it strengthened the perverse incentive to irrational and destructive behaviour. Even worse its use led inevitably to the prosecution and 'martyrdom' of individual trades unionists by legal proceedings in a special court which was easily devalued by smearing it as 'political' and not judicial in its origin and purpose. The legislation which I framed went to the roots of the problem by stripping away most of the immunities but leaving some, conditional upon the practice of democracy within the unions. Unions as corporate structures were forced to face the risk of civil actions by their own members if their rights were denied and by outsiders whose interests were wrongfully damaged. The refusal of Mrs Thatcher's Government to intervene to save companies or individuals from the consequence of destructive industrial disputes or pay settlements rendering labour costs uncompetitive, placed the responsibility for the welfare of businesses back on to the shoulders of management and, for their own welfare, on to the shoulders of individual workers.

Under the old regime it had been perfectly logical for workers in a powerful position relative to their employers (a category which included many public-sector workers willing to exploit a monopoly in essential services) to strike for higher pay for less output even if they were aware of the disastrous consequences for their firms or the national finances. Successive governments capitulated to blackmail by unions willing to inflict harm on vulnerable groups (schoolchildren, the sick and elderly) in pursuit of pay claims or entrenchment of their monopolies. Possible unemployment held no fear – large-scale unemployment was politically unacceptable so another job was around the corner even if the Government did not intervene to 'save' jobs. For the unskilled, unproductive and low-paid, unemployment meant little if any loss of net disposable income. For some in the public sector index-linked pay ensured that rising inflation meant a rising, not falling, standard of living. For others it was simply the platform for another pay claim. Again and again the lesson was rammed home. Militancy and resistance to higher productivity paid. Better pay came from obeying the instructions of union leaders – not those of employers.

Once the perverse incentive structure was abolished and a rational system put in its place, it was not long before rationality rather than apparent irrationality in industrial relations became the norm and the much talked about English disease – the incessant industrial stoppages and suicidal pay deals – was cured. Indeed the very expression has largely fallen out of use.

The old culture was replaced by a new one in which for the first time for many years productivity increases became an easier path to higher pay than strikes and go-slows. The welfare of the workforce became identified with the success of the employer and decoupled from the success or failure of the union. In consequence British manufacturing productivity increases outpaced those in Germany or even Japan bringing increases in real wages, profits and investment. What is surprising is not that this happened, but that so many politicians, economists and even business people should have been surprised that it did so. More recently some aspects of the disease threatened to return as excessive money supply and loose credit allowed businesses an excessively easy path to profitability without adequate cost control. This led to high inflation and flabby management responses to high pay demands in a labour market still artificially constrained by national pay bargaining, perverse wage/benefit relationships and poor skills training. Fortunately in its final phase Mrs Thatcher's Government and then that of John Major showed a willingness bordering on apparent political foolhardiness to risk severe recession to restate and reinforce the lessons of the new culture. The regression from industrial reality brought about by loss of monetary discipline certainly does not weaken the case for the 1980s union reforms. Rather does it strengthen the case both for those reforms and for prudent Thatcherite fiscal and monetary policies.

The learning process, the reorientation from the perverse system which had operated for at least 35 years, was extremely painful – particularly for slow learners. For example, the steel workers were wretchedly led by a generally decent and honourable union leadership and badly managed by an equally decent and honourable management unable to believe that the old Butskellite–Wilsonian–Heathite world had been swept aside. They stumbled into an appalling destructive strike from which it took even those whose jobs survived years to recover their financial losses. Many others followed suit.

In the private sector the recession combined with the slow response to the new environment destroyed many businesses. In the public sector there were more prolonged disputes since in such industries as water supply or hospital services, closures were not an option (although in coal-mining it was) and the official unemployment count soared to well over three million. In retrospect it is clear that the number of those genuinely without jobs and seeking work was far lower but nothing could take away from the needless human misery and economic cost involved in finally settling the bills run up during the post-war consensus in order to erect and maintain such a perverse system.

It is tragic that in the 1990–91 recession, brought about by the need to combat the high level of inflation, some of those lessons so painfully learned were forgotten and had to be re-learned. Had wages responded more quickly to the falling demand for labour, that fall and the recession would have been less deep and neither inflation nor unemployment need have gone so high.

One of the greatest assets of the market system is that the relationship between supply, demand and price is both logical and benign and, provided it is regulated against abuse, for example by monopoly or monopsony, it militates against politicians becoming involved. Even where politicians – and government agencies – do operate, human response is often dictated by market or quasi-market forces. For example where consumer choice is denied, price signals are suppressed or derided and monopoly power encouraged (as in education), costs go up, standards fall and consumers are abused. It matters little how much extra money is put into the market. The monopoly ensures that producers – or in some cases non-producers masquerading as, or hiding behind, the real producers – simply absorb the cash without any effect on quality and a disproportionately small effect on supply.

Where supply is not monopolised the effects of cash injection may be different. For example if the state advertises that young girls with children for whom no father is willing to take responsibility will be advantaged in terms of housing and income above other young unemployed or even the employed unskilled members of their peer group, there is a sharp increase in the supply of single-parent families. When sixteen-year-old children (many living in cramped conditions) are told that they have a right to homes of their own if they become homeless by walking out of the parental home, who can be surprised that homelessness increases sharply? Similarly if being classified as unemployed gives to particular individuals or families a higher net disposable income than relatively unskilled work then it should come as no surprise that some of those facing such a choice opt for unemployment.

Nor should one be surprised that if the cost of violently robbing, raping or taking the life of a fellow citizen is reduced, violent robbery, rape and murder become more widely spread.

If the road to hell is paved with good intentions it is certainly paved with bad intentions as well – but perhaps above all it is paved with soft options. And it has been a mixture of all three which led British society into the difficulties and tribulations of the post-war political consensus and the so-called permissive society. Equally the road to a better society is paved with good intentions and hard choices, some of which are set out in the following pages.

It is possible to take my theory a little further and to ask what sort of perverse social or political structure led to the construction of such a perverse system as the one I have described. The answer of the authoritarian is that we have an excessively democratic system and that of the paternalist that ordinary folk need to be protected from themselves by a benign elite establishment. In my view neither is the case. The fact is that humans are fallible, they often lack judgement and courage, and soft options are often the best options for those who will not be around to pay the bills when they are presented. The more that decision-making is centralised the more likely it is that there will be a ratchet effect of soft option succeeding soft option because that is easiest for those in authority. Burke observed, 'The individual is foolish but the species is wise.' That is an argument not for collectivism which centralises decision-making to a small number of individuals but for sep-arate decision-making by each member of the species and for economic and social systems sufficiently well designed to allow benign and constructive rewards to both individuals and the economy or society more generally. A collective response should be the sum of the response of each of the individuals concerned, not the imposition upon those individuals of a single centrally devised response. The former minimises and the latter maximises both the chance of serious error and the difficulty of rectifying such an error. The evolution of society, of industry and commerce, just as much as that of animal and plant life, requires the competition of ideas. Competition is confined, cabined, corrupted and distorted within a collectivist system but nurtured and fertilised within one which leaves individuals free to succeed – or just as important, to fail. It is the very basis of the common sense realistic approach which has become known as Thatcherism.

Unhappily, with the exception of the denationalisation of state industries and the reform of the law and practice of industrial relations, neither Thatcherism nor my own beliefs have yet been applied to the institutions and practices at the root of our economic and social problems.

The institutions crying out for reform are local government (dealt with alongside the constitution in Chapter 4), education, the health service and our cash-based welfare system.

Chief amongst the non-economic factors degrading British industrial performance are those rooted in our education system. The disdain for industry and commerce which has long been a feature of our educational establishment within public schools and universities is now partnered and supported by an outright hostility towards business, stemming from the modern left-wing public-sector education establishment. In addition the falling standards in the teaching profession and lowering of expectations of educational achievement have led to a particularly sharp decline in standards of teaching of science, mathematics and both English and foreign languages as well as of discipline and learning ability.

The poor condition of our state education system has at its roots the socialist-inspired egalitarian reforms of the 1960s and the flabby response of the Conservative establishment to the destruction of the grammar and technical schools. Whilst it would be absurd to represent the 1960s grammar, technical and secondary modern schools as perfect, that tripartite structure was soundly based on an ethos of academic excellence. Like the private sector, the grammar schools (and the direct grant schools) tended towards a somewhat narrow white-collar style in which science struggled to hold up its head to look the arts level in the eye and neither technology nor management skills had a place at all. The technical schools lacked resources – above all intellectual resources. At their worst they gave pupils only a second-rate foundation on which to build traditional (and often outdated) craft skill, yet they held the potential to become the preferred route for able would-be technologists and managers. Pupils with neither a technical bent nor the sharpness to take full advantage of the more hothouse intellectual climate of the grammar schools could find in the secondary modern schools something more suited to their style and abilities. Even so the best of such schools were well capable of taking pupils to good academic standards even if over a narrower range of subjects or at a slower pace.

The 1960s socialist ethos sought to slur over the distinction between failure and success. The quicker pupils had to be held back to accommodate the pace of the slowest. What could not be achieved by the many should be put beyond the reach of any. Under this pressure to exalt only the indifferent, not only schools changed but so did teachers and examinations. The search began for examinations, or to be more correct qualifications, which everyone could obtain, preferably without undue effort or knowledge. Achievement became devalued, discipline despised. Teachers sought to ape the behaviour and values of their pupils rather than to uphold the traditional high standards of personal conduct, knowledge and academic achievement. Literacy and numeracy began to take second place to 'self-fulfilment', 'creativity' and 'participation'. The egg-box culture and finger painting overshadowed basic literacy for five-year-olds. Everything had to be made 'easy' and entertaining, so arithmetical tables were discarded and reading taught by guessing rather than by understanding the structure of words. Needless to say teachers of quality could find little job satisfaction in such a system and were steadily replaced by ill-disciplined, intellectually lazy if not lacking, third-raters.

Despite the overwhelming evidence of falling standards a quite contrary picture is displayed by the architects of these disasters who point to statistics of ever-increasing examination success. Closer examination shows that the biggest examination cheats are not students but examiners, teachers and educationalists who simply water down standards to ensure that the appropriate quota of examinees achieve success. Those old enough to have standards by which to judge know full well that fewer and fewer students can perform simple arithmetical calculations involving fractions, or even decimals unless aided by a calculator, nor reliably and accurately add, subtract, multiply or divide, let alone use algebra, trigonometry or geometry. The English have always taken a practical, even cavalier attitude to spelling and grammar, rightly eschewing pedanticism in favour of meaning and impact. That has often enriched the language but many young school-leavers today are left unable to communicate effectively, especially in writing, for sheer ignorance of the structure of their own language.

Such an appalling decline was not wanted by the consumers of the education service. Learning has been long respected in England even by those who had little, and even more so in Wales and Scotland. The sad record could have been achieved only by a state-owned, producer-dominated near-absolute monopoly, operating alongside a highly competitive private sector to cater for the children of the elite and powerful establishment which was responsible for the provision of the public education it did not itself use. Steadily that establishment eliminated consumer choice and overrode public concern. Steadily, standards declined whilst quality control was eliminated, costs escalated and staff productivity fell. Indeed even after a decade of Thatcherism it remains a matter of pride amongst education ministers to claim that under their stewardship productivity has fallen and unit costs increased. These claims are usually expressed as 'an improving teacher-pupil ratio' and 'rising expenditure per pupil'. In any other business, managers are expected at least to try to raise quality standards, and to improve productivity of both labour and capital to reduce unit costs. In the world of commerce those who fail on all those counts would certainly be fired whilst in the world of state education they are acclaimed.

There is nothing inherently difficult in reversing these trends. Better education than we have today can be achieved at lower costs, although higher expenditure may well be needed to achieve the standards required for a high-wage, low-cost economy. But reforms must come first. Extra money poured into the present system is likely only to increase costs without affecting standards or volume of production. The task of reform is urgent. Already we have too many poorly educated and motivated products of the policies and practices of the seventies and eighties who will be not merely part of our workforce until the 2020s and 2030s, but the parents of another generation at risk and sadly the occupants of too many cells in our prisons.

Tragically the intellectually rigorous and right-thinking Sir Keith Joseph was unable to force his way through the political thicket nurtured by a quite untypically obstructive clique of civil servants, the prejudices of his colleagues, those of Members of Parliament of all parties and the self-centred arrogance of the educational establishment. Perhaps Keith Joseph was just too nice a man to drive through contentious reforms against unprincipled obstructionists and it is Kenneth Baker's Education Reform Act, although poorly constructed in parts and timorous in others, which sets out the road to reform and Kenneth Clarke who is the man most likely to drive along it. There is great hope and joy to be derived from the appointment of Professor Lord Griffiths to reconstruct the system of testing and assessment in schools and the overthrow of the establishment which had all but wrecked the attempt to make objective measurement of the success or failure of teachers in imparting knowledge to students. Mr Clarke's assessment should read, 'A good start, but much remains to be done.'

The concepts of choice for parents, de-monopolisation and de-politicisation of supply, alongside the setting of quality standards and quality control, whilst maintaining universal provision through state funding, are the foundation stones of the 1988 Act. More now needs to be built upon them. The major weaknesses of the Act are the system of opting out and the funding system for opted-out schools. There is a superficial attraction in leaving the decision whether or not to opt out to be made by parents and governors of schools. Certainly it made it easier to argue the case to allow the insertion of the thin edge of the wedge of consumer choice into the defensive wall of the educational establishment. However, the procedures for opting out and the unfair balance of power between the parents as consumers and the educational authorities and teaching unions as suppliers, ensure that only a small minority of schools will qualify to achieve grant-maintained status.

The pressing need is to accelerate and enlarge the programme by legislating a presumption that all schools should be opted out of local education authority control unless objectors can show good cause to the contrary. The argument that a school might not be viable should not be sufficient. Whether a school should survive or be closed should be for its users – not its employees or its municipal owners – and I have little doubt that faced with a choice between closure or the improvement of standards most schools would improve, and quickly too. Once the soft option of seeking extra resources by industrial misbehaviour and political lobbying was no longer open, teaching and administrative staff would in the vast majority of cases get on with the task of attracting resources by attracting parents to choose their particular schools.

The weakness of the present funding system is inherent in the very title of 'grant maintained school'. Schools should best be financed primarily by state payments in respect of pupils registered, bonuses for measured success (e.g. in examinations) and premiums for schools in deprived areas. Clearly if capital requirements are to be satisfied with minimum recourse to state grants, schools with vastly differing qualities of buildings and other capital would need to be given starting balance sheets to overcome such inequalities. After that, income streams from future fees could be used to finance borrowings from a state fund or indeed commercial sources, but schools should be given freedom to attract private-sector funding either by sponsorship, charitable donation or trading. The present under-use of valuable capital assets, meeting halls, seminar rooms, sports facilities and kitchens is a scandal which is tolerated only because they are controlled by arrogant monopolists. Freed from such control schools could not only raise cash to improve education but in doing so become far more valuable assets in the life of the communities within which they operate.

A school system of this kind would implant in the state sector the disciplines and incentives which have made the private sector sufficiently attractive to overcome the prejudices of many leading socialists who pay to educate their own children at private schools. It would allow choice to parents and encourage the ability of teachers to develop new methods and techniques to achieve traditional standards. Old assumptions, for example that high-quality teaching necessarily means a high teacher-pupil ratio, could be tested against such innovations as interactive computer-based learning systems. The claim by paternalists of both left and right that poor and badly educated families, especially those of non-British origin, do not aspire to higher standards for their children and are unfit to choose schools for them (which I reject) could also be put to the test.

A market for education such as this would require a two-way freedom. Freedom for parents to seek admission of their children to any school willing to accept them and freedom for schools to refuse any child, subject only to prohibition of unlawful discrimination. No doubt the choice of most parents would be influenced by subjective judgement and the practicalities of transport and distance, but objective information would be required if the market was to work efficiently. That judgement could be based primarily upon examination results but should be supplemented by the publication of DES inspectors' reports. Such reports would also form the basis of the judgement of the Secretary of State as to whether a school merited premium payments and whether its standards cleared the threshold below which fees would not be paid in respect of its pupils.

Defenders of the old status quo will maintain that many, if not most, parents are unfit to choose the school most suited to the needs and abilities of their children. That sits oddly with the freedom of parents, if they are sufficiently wealthy, to choose their children's school by buying a house within its catchment area, not to mention parents' democratic right to elect the members of the local authorities controlling the education authority which claims the right to know what is best for children.

There is no justification in principle nor practice for propping up an educational system which has demonstrably failed to educate adequately too many of our children either for work or to accept their responsibilities within society. The market system has clearly demonstrated its superiority over the centralised command system in supplying all manner of goods and services. The supply of education is far more important than that of package holidays, entertainment or electronic consumer goods and it is long overdue that it was liberated to meet the needs of its consumers.

It may well be that Mr Clarke's decision to transfer control of colleges of further education from local education authorities to their own management and thereby to their customers may have been precipitated by the search for a substitute for the community charge to help finance local government. For all that, it is educationally correct and has within it the potential to reorientate the colleges more firmly towards vocational education and training. It is to be hoped that having decided to sharply reduce the extent to which local government is financed by local taxation the Government will seize the chance to end the powers of councils to interfere in the provision of education. That provision currently accounts for forty-five per cent of total local government expenditure, and its transfer to central government funding should be part of the settlement of the introduction of the Council Tax to replace the community charge.

The advent of Youth Training Schemes began that process by developing a new market in which the colleges were able to sell their services. In consequence many colleges reorganised themselves, achieving forty-eight weeks of utilisation a year and offering new vocational training courses. If the funding system follows the principles advocated above for the schools sector then the colleges could play a major part in the much needed reform of training.

The Government's funding of universities is routed through the Universities Funding Council and (currently) the Polytechnics and Colleges Funding Council, with responsibility for the distribution of both capital and current expenditure grants falling to those councils. In addition there is direct funding to such institutions as the Open University and the Royal College of Art, and postgraduate awards, student loans and access funds for students particularly in need.

A recent change has been the introduction of tuition fees for first degree courses financed through the mandatory awards system to students, administered by Local Education Authorities but funded by central government.

Quite clearly there is little chance of 'market signals' being heard through the baffles and waffles created by such a system. In the more distant past when the universities catered only for a small generally wealthy elite they were well adapted to their purpose. However that form and structure, whilst it still has an important role to play, is not well suited to the role it is now asked to undertake; that is the teaching of specific business, industrial and scientific skills to first degree standard. In essence it is an extension of the school sixth form rather than something as different from school as was the pre-war university.

The problem was exacerbated by the Robins Report which led to many colleges of technology opting for university status and may be worsened still further by current proposals that polytechnics might follow the same route. Perhaps something is said about our social attitudes when the teaching of technology in specialist colleges seems to lack a status which can be gained only by calling the college a university and 'broadening' its role.

There are no easy short routes to persuade our large university sector that it is spending too much time, money and intellectual capital on teaching subjects lacking in market appeal to the employers who will provide jobs for young graduates and the wealth to sustain the universities. Again there is a system of perverse incentives. The standing of a university is affected by the quality of undergraduates it attracts and their number. Sadly, many of the 'hard' skills, engineering for example, are expensive to teach (or to research) and many of those with least commercial appeal are the cheapest to teach. An institution seeking to grow, or to attract government finance through the UFC is bound therefore to be tempted to maximise its student intake and minimise the cost of their education by skewing the curricula towards skills in lesser commercial demand.

In my view it would be helpful if much greater incentive was given to persuade commerce and industry to sponsor students. Tax deductability is of less value as corporate tax rates fall and some new incentive, perhaps 100 per cent rebate of the cost is needed. Provided the sponsorship was for an amount sufficient to disqualify the recipient from state maintenance grant, the cost to the Exchequer would be no greater, but the benign influence would be considerable. The brightest young men and women would tend to be attracted to the most generous sponsorships. Institutions seeking to attract those bright young people would have to excel in the disciplines favoured by the sponsors. Thus an indirect pressure, a well-modulated market signal would be received or felt by the universities. The students would of course benefit from the interest shown in their progress by their sponsors, and be aware that they were being paid by business to study, and the sponsors would naturally be drawn into a closer relationship with universities.

A change of this kind, together with a more overt government policy to achieve greater funding for universities successfully attracting such undergraduates and teaching 'expensive' skills, would over a period change the motivation of academics. These proposals would not, nor would they be intended to, reduce universities to teaching factories. No doubt many major employers recognising the value of a classically rounded education in business would sponsor across a wide range of disciplines and the state itself would continue to fund a substantial proportion of students. For my part I would welcome a degree of overt discrimination by differential grants according to disciplines, which could also encourage humanities and arts as commercially important skills but above all would have a sense of direction.

It might be thought radical, even crude and uncultured to talk of market signals in education. However, to introduce such ideas into health care is to risk being abused as not merely cruel, grasping, materialistic and unfeeling but actually blasphemous to suggest that the NHS is divided from perfection by anything except money.

Yet at its roots the concept of the National Health Service is no more than that health care should be available at the time of need and without charge, the costs being centrally borne out of taxation. Give or take a little – treatment for non-urgent needs has seldom been available on demand without delay across the board and charges for drugs and appliances have long been established – that concept has survived unscathed and has never been at risk. Essentially it is a compulsory universal health insurance scheme in which the premiums are related to ability to pay through the general burden of taxation. Unlike many other services provided by public authorities, whilst demand is extremely uneven as between one citizen and another it is less influenced by income, social class or region than by age.

The benefit in terms of charge-free services can be quite small for some individuals and it would be comfortably within their ability to pay, but for others the costs may be beyond the resources of all but the substantially wealthy, and no one knows if or when they might suddenly be removed from the first category into the second. In addition demand is overwhelmingly a matter of need rather than choice.

In all these respects, and others too, the financing of health care is probably best left to be met largely, although not entirely, by universal state funding. Within this context arguments for a move to the French system under which patients broadly pay for treatment and are then almost completely reimbursed, or to payment for the hotel or board and lodging element of hospital in-patient care, are peripheral. Substantial sums might be raised by such schemes to reduce the cost to the Exchequer. However, the need for means-tested exemptions adds complication and cost as well as political problems which I think are best put to one side in the interest of concentration on the more important issue of the delivery of high-quality health care at minimum cost.

It comes as a surprise to many people today to discover that although we had no NHS before 1947 health care was widely available even to the poor through general practitioners, largely charitable hospitals and sickness insurance schemes. The NHS as introduced by the post-war Labour Government not only contained the concept of universally available, centrally funded care without charge but it also nationalised the hospitals and brought general practitioners into a curious status of self-employment with dependence on state funding.

In retrospect it can be seen that hospital nationalisation and the growth of the regional and district health authorities was a mistake. Many reforms of that system have been attempted but its inherent weaknesses remain. It is an essentially top-down system allowing patients, customers, consumers, clients or whatever name we give to its users, little choice or influence. It has been dominated by producers, managed and funded not least by response to political pressures. Money has flowed towards the best organised lobby not the greatest need, nor to where any given sum would alleviate the greatest amount of suffering.

In the heady post-war days of 1945 it was generally accepted that state-financed preventative medicine, better housing and a rising standard of living would combine to so improve health that the costs of the NHS would peak and then fall. In fact the progress of medicine has created a demand which, if not infinite, has no boundaries or limits yet in sight. There is no foreseeable time at which sufficient resources of money – or indeed people – will be available to meet the constantly growing demand created by the constantly growing ability of the medical profession to improve health care. Indeed, the more that is spent on research the greater the demand for cash to finance new treatments, and the more successful we are in extending the average lifespan, the greater the demand for medical services for the elderly.

The political rows over the health service have a substantially bogus element to them. The Labour Party denounces the Conservative Government for denying or delaying treatment to those in need of it by providing insufficient money to the NHS. Asked, however, if a Labour Government would finance the NHS on a demand basis without a cash limit, Labour's spokesmen after much squirming admit that health care would be cash limited. Nothing will drag from the spokesmen any intimation of what that cash limit would be but within the context of promises and undertakings and implications that staff pay would be greatly increased, and the search for efficiency abandoned, there would seem little prospect of more or better treatment without expenditure increases well beyond the ability of the economy to bear. The party arguments about spending are therefore irrelevant. What matters is not input but output and the Conservative Government has mismanaged the debate on the NHS, first by using the rhetoric of hard-faced cutters of expenditure whilst they greatly increased spending and then arguing with the Labour Party on a 'we spend more than you did' basis, before finally moving to the only important criterion of 'we treat more people better than you did'.

It ought to be clear that the debate should be first and above all about which system and structure is most likely to maximise the amount of health care delivered per pound of expenditure and to ensure that care is delivered to where it will alleviate the most suffering. The decision on how much money should be spent is a separate matter which cannot be simply decided within the context of a debate about the NHS but only within a wider debate on the economy and other demands upon it. This is not a matter of putting cash before care. Cash has to be provided before care can be provided, so cash comes first in the debate and in the management of the country and the NHS.

There is comfort to be found in the gradual and stumbling but none the less perceptible movement of the Labour leadership towards neo-realism which led Mr Kinnock, when interviewed in April 1991 by Mr Brian Walden, to say that a Labour government would not increase expenditure on the NHS until economic growth provided increased resources to do so. If this glimmer of light in the darkness of socialist thinking should grow to illuminate the shoddy structure of the Party's fatuous rhetoric on the NHS it might be possible for there to be an intelligent debate on this issue for the first time in almost half a century.

Until April 1991 once a cash limit for the hospital services had been agreed in the light of the state of the economy and of all other demands for Government expenditure, that money for both capital and revenue expenditure was distributed by Ministers to Area Health Authorities who then distributed down to District and individual units. Expenditure through the general practitioner service is not generally of itself cash-limited but in practice the size of that expenditure is not entirely out of the minds of Ministers as they consider the totality of health expenditure.

That process was guided, perhaps influenced is a better word, by all manner of considerations. Formally it all flowed from the work of RAWP – the Resource Allocation Working Party – whose objectivity has not unnaturally been challenged by all areas receiving less than they held to be their right. Certainly no one should underestimate the lobbying weight of senior medical staff and groups seeking cash for particular hospitals or areas of medicine. The reforms leading towards an internal market and particularly the creation of trust hospitals within the NHS initiated by Mr Kenneth Clarke are beginning to affect this process. There is no doubt that the concept of making district health authorities into purchasing authorities buying treatment for patients from hospitals is correct, although it cannot entirely obviate the need to allocate cash to regions and on down to districts. The problem is the slowness of this change. The producer interest of NHS employees, more than a million in total, is being defended in depth, no doubt encouraged by its success in stalling and destroying earlier attempts at reform.

My conclusion is that a much more radical approach is needed. This would be designed to remove most of the bureaucratic non-operational structures currently on top of the hospitals. At present that structure has not only the function of distribution of cash but the broad planning of provision. Those functions must continue to be carried out and the broad planning and assessment of likely future needs is essentially a top down process since it depends upon a long look forward at trends outside the remit of the NHS, for example regional population growth. That points to the continuation of a regional structure with the principal mechanism for the distribution of cash to existing units being closely related to short and medium demand by a market mechanism.

The current reforms go a long way along this path and the self-governing trust hospitals largely satisfy the need. But for the system to work so effectively as to allow the virtual elimination of a wide range of health authority administrative functions all hospitals need to become self-governing trading units either in their own right or as part of a group. Their cash needs would then be supplied solely by treating patients under contract, and by contracting to the Government to supply services such as casualty centres and by raising money outside the NHS. There would have to be a governmental function (as indeed there is now) governing the boundaries of what treatments were available within the NHS. Whether cosmetic surgery should be available without charge is essentially a political rather than a clinical decision. More difficult is the decision of when new techniques or treatments should become freely available. Here, once again, this problem is not new as demonstrated by the making available of hip replacement and organ transplant surgery in recent years.

Quite clearly there is a need for some more rational way of determining which potential new techniques should be financed. This is not because money available for medical research and development is itself limited but because since resources are not infinite they should be directed to where the greatest alleviation of suffering might be achieved for the money available for treatment. It is not sufficient justification for the development of a new technique or treatment that it is possible to achieve and that it would benefit some patients. Rather should there be an attempt to direct resources to where new techniques might be expected to lower the cost and therefore widen the availability of treatments for specific conditions, or to open up the possibility of the treatment within available resources for patients for whom little can at present be done.

Uncomfortable as it would be, I believe that Ministers, administrators and the medical profession should be required to face up to the need to choose, for example, between money for further development of extremely expensive techniques highly satisfying to the professional instincts of the doctors concerned, but of use to a very limited number of patients and perhaps less exciting, less glamorous developments likely to alleviate suffering of large numbers of people. There is little doubt in my mind that amongst the most neglected area of both research and treatment today is that of mental illness, yet in human or economic terms it must be an area of the very greatest need. Unhappily depression, schizophrenia, even senile dementia, and other mental illnesses are, like rehabilitation, less exciting fields than organ transplant and are starved of resources.

The day-to-day issues of resource distribution are less difficult and more open to market solutions. It is certainly not the easiest thing in the world, but it is proving entirely possible to arrive at prices to set alongside the menu of treatments and for health authorities to act as the buying agents on behalf of the practitioner making the referral. Of course hospitals would wish to bid also for contracts to supply services such as major casualty units to be available for a disaster level of demand on a 365 days a year basis. But their income for all current and a large part of capital expenditure should be financed by normal treatment under contracts. Capital for major developments could be made available on similar lines to that which I propose for schools from a government loan fund. There is no evidence that this would constitute an excessive management or administrative demand on NHS hospitals any more than it does on those in the private sector. It would provide a powerful incentive for a downward pressure on costs and an upward pressure on quality and it could allow NHS patients to be treated in the private sector if that was able to offer competitive service.

Until Kenneth Clarke's reforms are fully carried through, hospitals which set out to treat more patients to higher standards, using the investment which has been made in their facilities to the fullest extent, are likely to continue to run out of money and join the list of NHS bad boys as over-spenders. Until now, hospitals which under-used the capital invested in them and which closed wards and turned away patients have been likely to be put into the 'good boy' category for living within their cash limits. Even worse, when further capital investment was being decided upon it has been likely that the 'good boy' hospital which is making poor use of its existing capital stock would be favoured. Could a more perverse system be designed?

At the root of this perversity was the misapplication to the NHS of a government accounting system which for good reasons writes off capital as it is spent and makes no charge for it in its current accounts. In a business, and the NHS is a business, this renders proper cost comparisons (which are a vital tool of management) quite impossible to make.

The structure of such a new system might eventually take a number of different forms. The optimum could emerge only from experience of the Clarke reforms, a great deal of consultation and perhaps pilot schemes covering more than one health region. However, it would most likely follow a pattern in which the district authority acted as purchasing agent and the regional authority acted as a strategic advisory body through which applications for access to the NHS capital loan fund would be made. Clearly the role and perhaps membership of the Medical Research Council would be affected and the guidance given to it would need to be reviewed. The importance of the reforms I advocate, however, would not rest upon particular structures but upon the principles of treatment without charge, more purposeful direction of research and the use of market mechanisms and commercial management practices to ensure the maximum of benefit to patients from every pound of NHS expenditure.

In a world in which even the Labour Party has been reluctantly driven to the rational conclusion that there will be financial constraints upon the NHS, no one, not even medical professions, can be allowed to shrug off their responsibility to ensure the optimum use of whatever resources are made available. I do not believe that either the travelling public or professional engineers within the aerospace industry have suffered because such disciplines have been imposed within a regulatory system which has set out the standards to be observed, and nor would patients or medical professionals do so if similar disciplines were practised within health care. Indeed many professionals would find their work assisted and their authority enhanced whilst patients would gain from a higher quality of overall care.

The reform of our education and health care systems are no longer universally regarded as impossible or undesirable, although it is fair to say that those perceptions are not yet universally held. Gradually, as the prospect of simply pouring in more and more resources (the NHS now spends 50 per cent more in real terms than just over a decade ago) in the hope of curing all ills fades, the professional teaching and medical staff are becoming reconciled to tackling their problems by better resource management. In doing so they are discovering to their astonishment that it leads to higher quality as well as greater output. That process is now under way and one is no longer necessarily regarded as a dangerous, even unbalanced, radical for questioning the existing system and advocating change.

The debate on welfare is not yet at such an advanced stage. In general the subject is still regarded as too hot to handle. The charge that anyone wishing to change the education system without the permission of the NUT, or the NHS without the approval of NUPE, COSHE, RCN and BMA, is seeking to abolish free education or health care no longer inhibits would-be reformers, and will have less and less credence with the voters at large. Those who speak or write about welfare (except to advocate more and more expenditure within the existing system), however, can expect little but spiteful abuse. None the less a system which now consumes a quarter of all public expenditure, some £58 billion in 1990/91 when the whole yield of income tax was less than £56 billion, yet fails to deal with obvious poverty can hardly be allowed to drift on, costing more each year but doing no more than drip feed an army of those unable or unwilling to support themselves.

The history of attempted and achieved reforms during Mrs Thatcher's premiership has been mixed. Every review has first stirred then disappointed Treasury hopes that the haemorrhage of money through the benefit system might be diminished. Each reform – however large the increase in resources – has led to ever more accusations of an intent to grind the faces of the poor into the very dust, regardless of fact or reason.

Much good has come from such reviews. For example, the position of the long term sick and disabled has improved with increases of more than half a million in both those receiving attendance allowance and mobility allowance; of almost 600,000 in those on invalidity benefit and over 100,000 on invalidity pension and severe disablement allowance. Expenditure on these categories alone is now over £10 billion (an increase of 126 per cent) with substantial further expenditure planned over the next three years. None the less, reviews and changes in the scope, shape and extent of welfare benefits have satisfied neither beneficiaries, the Treasury nor the poverty industry. The latter would of course be the most difficult of those three groups to satisfy for it lives, and lives increasingly well, on the plight of the poor. Although the industry has grown from numerous organisations of selfless and good people (many, if not most, volunteers) and still contains many of them within it, it is now dominated by a different group who depend upon it for their living as much as workers at Ford or Rover depend upon the car industry. For them the adage that the poor will always be with us is an assurance of both a living and a platform for their views on the ills and shortcomings of society.

I have not approached the problems of poverty and the welfare business from the Treasury's point of view. Very rightly the Treasury has been concerned with what goes in by way of cash, but in my view has not devoted enough thought to the value which has been achieved by that expenditure. Few of those who have experienced poverty themselves would wish it upon others, but a good many of us realise that whilst a drip feed of benefit in cash or kind alleviates the symptoms it does little to attack the cause, or to offer individuals a path out of poverty itself. Indeed there is a strong case to be made that the long-term effect of even a half adequate benefit system of the kind we have today is likely to worsen, not ease, the underlying problem. Those who experienced poverty twenty, thirty or even fifty years ago, or even those who have studied poverty over the years, are acutely conscious that what is now regarded as life on or close to the poverty line would have been an enviable state of security for many people half a century ago. The point is underlined by those who would set the poverty line, and benefits too, on some percentage or other of average earnings and concede, indeed uphold, the idea that our view of what constitutes poverty should be lifted as the general standard of living rises. Oddly such people mostly bridle at the contention that poverty is a relative, not an absolute concept.

The radical looking at these problems is bound to ask not only what is poverty but who are its victims and why cannot they escape, either unaided or with help, from its grip.

At one time in this land and still in much of the world today poverty meant no more nor less than an insufficiency of food, water, shelter and clothing securely to sustain life. Such a definition in a country so wealthy as Great Britain is clearly unacceptable, yet once it is discarded one is inevitably adrift in a sea of subjective and ephemeral judgements. I do not believe it sensible to postulate some mechanical linkage of relativities to average standards or incomes, but I have to accept that there is at any time some kind of collective judgement of the minimum standard of life which a fellow citizen should be guaranteed. However, it seems to me that such a standard is now so far above mere subsistence that it should embrace a differential between those unable through age, infirmity or incapacity to provide for themselves and those who could, but choose not to do so.

The need of such a concept becomes clear as one looks at who are the victims of poverty. The most obvious groups are to be found amongst the elderly, many of whom are deprived of the opportunity to work by prejudice, social convention, restrictive practice or infirmity and who had little chance in their earlier years to acquire savings or adequate pension rights. A second category comprises the long term sick and physically disabled and those intellectually inadequate for unsheltered employment. Sadly, there is a growing population of children in families lacking one parent and thereby without a bread-winner, due to death, illness, desertion, or to the fecklessness or choice of their mothers. Unemployment is a common feature of all those categories but there is a further group whose poverty arises solely from unemployment. That may be subdivided into those willing (and generally eager) to resume work but for whom no job is available and those who have rejected work as a way of life and are willing to accept a low standard of living so long as it can be achieved in idleness.

There seems little reason for society to guarantee any growth in living standards – or indeed anything beyond soup kitchen and hostel maintenance – to those who wilfully without cause decline to contribute to their own maintenance or the national production of wealth. Beyond that, whilst decent standards should be maintained for the less fortunate it would seem particularly perverse to link benefit to wage levels. After all, if by any combination of workforce militancy or management stupidity, excessive pay rises are achieved resulting in the closure of businesses, the unemployment of their workers and thereby a reduction in wealth within the economy, it would be odd, indeed insupportable, if welfare benefits should increase in consequence.

Nor should one be insensitive to the dangers of providing a

standard of living for (for example) young women who have recklessly become mothers without a breadwinning partner which is little different from that achieved in unskilled work by their sisters. Children born into, and brought up in, dependence upon welfare benefits are, I suspect, particularly vulnerable to falling into the same trap as their parents. Whilst society has a duty to protect such children from the consequences of the follies, selfishness, improvidence or fecklessness of their parents it also has a duty not to widen the circle of deprivation by rewarding such behaviour and thereby encouraging others to emulate it.

There is no perfect all-embracing answer to these problems, and attempts to find one are all too likely to create new perverse incentives as they bring relief to those already in need. However, despite my earlier doubts I have been driven to the conclusion that the basic form of income support should now rest upon a workfare system of the kind advocated by Ralph Howell MP.

Much abuse has been heaped on Ralph Howell and the other early advocates of workfare. His ideas have been condemned not only by the prime beneficiaries of the present system, those employed in and who gain their living from the poverty industry, but what one might generally call the Treasury lobby which has ruled out workfare as too expensive. The most bitter attacks have come from those who choose to style themselves as protectors of the inheritance of Professor Beveridge whose famous report *Social Insurance and Allied Services* of 1942 was the foundation of what became known as the Welfare State. Like many self avowed disciples of Keynes, those who claim to uphold the doctrines of Beveridge are remarkably selective in their reading of his work. Indeed from the earliest days of implementation of his reforms the political pressures were to accept and implement the give away items and to ignore the caveats, cautions and restrictions.

The three guiding principles of Beveridge were, first, that to deal with the problems of what he called social insurance required a fresh start with a new system, not merely a 'patching' of the old. Second, social insurance should be only part of a programme of reform. In his words, 'it is an attack upon want. But Want is only one of five giants on the road of reconstruction and in some ways the easiest to attack. The others are Disease, Ignorance, Squalor and Idleness.' His third principle was that 'social security must be achieved by cooperation between the State and the individual. The State should offer security for service and contribution, not stifle incentive, opportunity, responsibility; in establishing a national minimum it should leave room and encouragement for voluntary action by each individual to provide more than that minimum for himself and his family.' I would not differ from Beveridge in any of that, nor indeed from what he went on to say but which was sadly ignored:

> It [his report] is, first and foremost, a plan of insurance – of giving in return for contributions benefits up to subsistence level as of right and without means testing, so that individuals may build freely upon it.

The concept of insurance – of benefits in return for contributions – was soon lost. Had it not been, the brake on expenditure would have been applied not by the Treasury, but by the contributors. Nor has the concept of 'subsistence level' payments lasted, let alone that they should be paid without means testing.

We have certainly drifted a long way from Beveridge, erecting a system from which almost all of the balance he proposed has been removed. Who now calls for the individual to offer 'service' as well as 'contribution' in return for benefit? One can imagine the shocked tones of the ever impartial BBC interviewer, let along the waspish and sanctimonious poverty lobby spokesman, should a Conservative spokesman say that the claimant for unemployment benefit 'should not feel that income for idleness, however caused, can come from a bottomless purse'. No doubt such people would support the view of Beveridge that in return for that understanding the Government should accept 'the major responsibility of seeing that unemployment and disease are reduced to the minimum' but their feeling of shock might return if that Conservative spokesman, like Beveridge, accepted $8\frac{1}{2}$ per cent as the normal average rate of unemployment. Even greater shock was caused when Lord Young, as Employment Secretary, moved very slightly towards Beveridge's view that 'conditions must be imposed at some stage or another as to how men in receipt of benefit shall use their time, so as to fit themselves or to keep themselves fit for service'.

In the 1980s, however, it was thought unwise to quote the no-nonsense comment in the 1942 Report that such conditions would be 'the most effective way of unmasking malingerers'. As Employment Secretary at a time of sharply rising unemployment I did not feel able to do more than begin to prepare the ground for a return to Lord Beveridge's view that 'The danger of providing benefits, which are both adequate in amount and indefinite in duration' is 'that men as creatures who adapt to circumstances may settle down to them.'

Indeed I became the target of much abuse when I introduced the Youth Training Scheme which ensured that all young school leavers of sixteen unable to find jobs would be offered training places, initially for twelve months. The accusations included allegations that I was seeking to introduce industrial conscription, forced labour, even slavery. The abuse reached its hysterical crescendo at my suggestion that youngsters who preferred unemployment (idleness, as Beveridge put it more bluntly) to training should not receive benefit. Yet on page 58 the 1942 Report wisely recommended that 'for boys and girls there should ideally be no unconditional benefit at all; their enforced abstention from work should be made an occasion for further training'.

On re-reading Lord Beveridge's work one is struck by its overwhelming common sense, humanity and realism. His words on the nature of what he calls social insurance (p. 11, para. 21) are exceptionally wise:

> 21. The first view is that benefit in return for contributions, rather than free allowances from the State, is what the people of Britain desire. This desire is shown both by the established popularity of compulsory insurance, and by the phenomenal growth of voluntary insurance against sickness, against death and for endowment, and most recently for hospital treatment. *It is shown in another way by the strength of popular objection to any kind of means test. This objection springs not so much from a desire to get everything for nothing, as from resentment, at a provision which appears to penalise what people have come to regard as the duty and pleasure of thrift, of putting pennies away for a rainy day.* Management of one's income is an essential element of a citizen's freedom. Payment of a substantial part of the cost of benefit as a contribution irrespective of the means of the contributor is the firm basis of a claim to benefit irrespective of means. [Italics added.]

In my view few things have so undermined the willingness of those on modest incomes to save as the realisation that in times of need, not least in retirement, their prudence is penalised and they find themselves no better off than those who could have, but chose not to, save to provide for future needs.

Beveridge argued that benefits should be provided by the insurance system with an identifiable fund from which they would be paid. Again, as we hear the cheap promises of the current generation of huckster politicians promising even higher and more widely available benefits without cost to the recipients, it is refreshing to read Beveridge setting out his case as follows (p. 12, para. 22):

> **22.** The second view is that whatever money is required for provision of insurance benefits, so long as they are needed, should come from a Fund to which the recipients have contributed and to which they may be required to make larger contributions if the Fund proves inadequate. The plan adopted since 1930 in regard to prolonged unemployment and sometimes suggested for prolonged disability, that the State should take this burden off insurance, in order to keep the contribution down, is wrong in principle. The insured persons should not feel that income for idleness, however caused, can come from a bottomless purse. The Government should not feel that by paying doles it can avoid the major responsibility of seeing that unemployment and disease are reduced to the minimum. The place for direct expenditure and organisation by the State is in maintaining employment of the labour and other productive resources of the country, and in preventing and combating disease, not in patching an incomplete scheme of insurance.

The influence of Keynesian thinking is clear enough in the reference to the responsibility of the State for the maintenance of a high level of employment, but so too is the thinking of Burke. To my mind there has never been any doubt about the responsibility of Government, in that matter, but the logic of sober realism dictates that avoidance of mass unemployment (even taking the Beveridge definition of an average level of $8\frac{1}{2}$ per cent through the economic cycle) cannot be achieved by the State alone. It requires not only a rigorous control of inflation by government but the operation of vigorous competitive and profitable manufacturing and service industries by business, with heavy responsibility upon the providers both of capital and labour.

In re-reading Beveridge I find myself time and time again unequivocally on his side and unequivocally opposed to much of what has been done in his name over the past fifty years. Who would not agree with him that (pages 57 and 58, paras. 129 and 130):

> ... the existing provisions for dealing with prolonged interruption of earnings are unsatisfactory. For disability the cash benefit is drastically reduced, though the needs have almost certainly increased; for unemployment the insured person is referred from benefit to assistance, which may give him higher, or lower, or equal income, but will give it subject to a means test, and normally will do nothing but give an income. The needs of persons suffering from prolonged unemployment or disability are; on the one hand, for as much income at least as before, without any means test discouraging voluntary provision, and, on the other hand, for the taking of steps to prevent deterioration and encourage recovery. It is proposed, accordingly, that the rates both for unemployment and for disability should continue without diminution so long as unemployment or disability lasts; this abolishes the present distinction between sickness and disablement benefits under health insurance.
>
> **130.** To reduce the income of an unemployed or disabled person, either directly or by application of a means test, because the unemployment or disability has lasted for a certain period, is wrong in principle. But it is equally wrong to ignore the fact that to make unemployment or disability benefit, which is adequate for subsistence, also indefinite in duration involves a danger against which practical precautions must be taken. Most men who have once

gained the habit of work would rather work – in ways to which they are used – than be idle, and all men would rather be well than ill. But getting work or getting well may involve a change of habits, doing something that is unfamiliar or leaving one's friends or making a painful effort of some other kind. The danger of providing benefits, which are both adequate in amount and indefinite in duration, is that men, as creatures who adapt themselves to circumstances, may settle down to them. In the proposals of the present Report, not only are insurance benefits being made for the first time adequate for subsistence without other means, but the possibility of drawing them is being extended to new classes not hitherto accustomed to industrial discipline. The correlative of the State's undertaking to ensure adequate benefit for unavoidable interruption of earnings, however long, is enforcement of the citizen's obligation to seek and accept all reasonable opportunities of work, to co-operate in measures designed to save him from habituation to idleness, and to take all proper measures to be well. The higher the benefits provided out of a common fund for unmerited misfortune, the higher must be the citizen's sense of obligation not to draw upon that fund unnecessarily.

Nor is it easy to disagree with the conclusions which were drawn (in para. 131) from the impeccable analysis:

131. This general principle leads to the following practical conclusions:
(i) Men and women in receipt of unemployment benefit cannot be allowed to hold out indefinitely for work of the type to which they are used or in their present places of residence, if there is work which they could do available at the standard wage for that work.

(ii) Men and women who have been unemployed for a certain period should be required as a condition of continued benefit to attend a work or training centre, such attendance being designed both as a means of preventing habituation to idleness and as a means of improving capacity for earning. Incidentally, though this is an altogether minor reason for the proposal, such a condition is the most effective way of unmasking the relatively few persons who may be suspected of malingering, who have perhaps some concealed means of earning which they are combining with an appearance of unemployment. The period after which attendance should be required need not be the same at all times or for all persons. It might be extended in times of high unemployment and reduced in times of good employment; six months for adults would perhaps be a reasonable average period of benefit without conditions. But for young persons who have not yet the habit of continuous work the period should be shorter; for boys and girls there should ideally be no unconditional benefit at all; their enforced abstention from work should be made an occasion of further training.

(iii) The measures for control of claims to disability benefit – both by certification and by sick visiting – will need to be strengthened, in view of the large increases proposed in the scale of compulsory insurance benefit and the possibility of adding to this substantially by voluntary insurance through Friendly Societies.

(iv) Special attention should be paid to the prevention of chronic disability, by intensified treatment, advice and supervision of cases in which it is threatened and by research into its causes.

(v) Conditions imposed on benefit must be enforced where necessary by suitable penalties.

Bringing the 1942 analysis up to date in the light of life in the 1990s strengthens rather than weakens the conclusions. Beveridge could hardly have envisaged the racket in the provision of false passports and other documents to illegal immigrants attracted by the prospect of easy living without work to a standard far higher than work (even if available) would provide in their countries of origin. Clearly a passport bringing entitlement to cash benefits has a price – indeed two passports bringing twice the benefit clearly has double the value and it should come as no surprise that the trade exists. Nor amongst nationals of the countries concerned is there anything remarkable in the trade – all state documents are for sale in most of the third world.

For those unable to pay so much in cash to enter the benefit scheme the traditional illegal entry routes are an alternative, but cheaper still and more likely to succeed is the political asylum racket. Increasingly nationals of countries torn apart by the famine, civil wars, corruption and incompetence endemic in many third world countries claim to be victims of political persecution seeking asylum in Britain and other capitalist Western nations with generous welfare systems. At worst they are likely to enjoy life in Britain for a year or so before being deported. In fact many are allowed to stay permanently because formally or informally the difficult process of deportation is simply given up. In short the category of people identified by Beveridge (para. 130) of 'new classes not hitherto accustomed to industrial discipline' and therefore potentially liable to accept life on benefit without work as a way of life is vastly larger than he feared.

Over the past fifty years other attitudes have changed – many just as Beveridge feared that they might without proper controls. I suspect he would have been shocked by the idea of Claimants Unions, of a society obsessed with rights and dismissive of obligations. Fraud and dishonesty were far from unknown at all levels of society before the Second World War but if detected they were punished not only through the judicial system but by the shame which society heaped upon those concerned. These days the benefit fraudster is as likely to be depicted as a sympathetic – even heroic – character as a shameful cheat stealing from his fellows.

It is a matter for debate whether the contributory insurance concept of funding the main welfare benefits could be re-created. For myself I see no objections in principle, and some prospect in practice of simply cutting income tax to balance a more realistic national insurance contribution and it is certain that cash benefits could be financed in that way. However, the steady increase in the number of those with an entitlement to non-state pensions (including in that loose definition, state employees with occupational pension rights) has been rising rapidly. Retired people are therefore becoming less reliant upon the state pension which is unfunded and paid by current taxpayers making it progressively easier to freeze its real value and the cost burden which has to be borne out of taxation.

In the early 1940s there was a widespread fear (shared by Beveridge) that Britain's population was in serious long-term decline due to a declining birth rate. In his words,

> ... unless this rate [of reproduction] is raised very materially in the near future a rapid and continuous decline of the population cannot be prevented ... [this] makes it imperative to give first place in social expenditure to the care of childhood and to the safeguarding of maternity [p. 18, para. 15].

Beveridge was not so foolish as to see the children's allowances which he proposed as being a direct incentive towards larger families amongst lower paid workers. Certainly the case which is made for child benefit today is not that we need to raise our birth rate, but that many children would live in poverty without cash from the state. However, at the other end of the age spectrum today's problem is the same as that of 1942. That is the 'age constitution of the population' which made it 'certain that persons past the age that is now regarded as the end of working life will be a much larger proportion of the whole community than at any time in the past'. This 'makes it necessary to seek ways of postponing the age of retirement from work rather than of hastening it'.

Throughout my time as Secretary of State for Employment I struggled against the pressure to bring down the retirement age (i.e. to pay a full state retirement pension at an earlier age) and only just managed to hold the line by offering various temporary early retirement schemes. Even now, despite the obvious adverse economic and social effects the pressure continues, fuelled not least by the bureaucratic obsession of the European Community with standardisation and so-called sexual equality – by which they mean uniformity imposed upon the non-uniform.

None of the considerations in the mind of Beveridge as he wrote his report are irrelevant today. Need is concentrated amongst the elderly, large families and the long-term unemployed as it was sixty years ago although since then single-parent families have become a major problem and the numbers of predominantly younger people openly hostile to the idea of working for a living has sharply increased.

I believe that the perverse incentives against which Beveridge warned have now become so deeply embedded in the structure of our welfare system which has in turn corrupted large sections of the community that we must change course sharply to return to the spirit of the 1942 Report.

The basic form of future income-support schemes should rest upon workfare. The scheme most recently proposed by Ralph Howell MP is based upon the concept that the state should be the employer of last resort, not the provider of last resort. Workfare, he says, does not involve compulsion but simply invokes the principle that those without normal employment should be able to work. In his most recent study Mr Howell proposed that as employer of last resort the state should offer a basic wage of £2.50 per hour for up to forty hours work, making £100 per week with lower rates for those under 20. In Howell's scheme those able bodied people who chose not to work would receive nothing. On the other hand those choosing to work less than forty hours would be paid pro rata. At the same time the income-tax threshold would be raised to £100 for a single person and £150 for a married couple with a starting rate of 25 per cent. Currently the threshold is £63.36 for a single person and £96.44 for a couple. These changes, which would cost something approaching £10 billion, would be financed by an increase in the higher rate of tax to 50 per cent and higher indirect taxes including VAT.

Against that Howell believes (and I agree with him) that such a system would sharply reduce the numbers registered as unemployed. In addition progressive change to an insurance based system with higher national insurance charges could obviously reduce the impact on income tax or VAT.

It is of course a poor way to justify new public expenditure by pointing to other large expenditures which have been undertaken for different purposes. None the less it is not unreasonable to recollect that the introduction of YTS involved an initial expenditure of some £1 billion and Community Programme some £350 million, not to mention the decision to cut community charge bills by £140 a head at a cost of well over £4 billion. Some of Howell's critics claim that the introduction of workfare would amount to the introduction of a minimum wage. That is no more and no less true than that any cash benefit to the unemployed establishes a wage floor. More important is the level of the floor and Howell's £2.50 contrasts with the £3.75 which Labour's proposals would currently require.

Perhaps the more serious doubts about workfare revolve not around financing its wage bill but the practicability of organising a work force which might exceed two million people and providing resources of materials, etc. with which they would work. That would require changing some deeply entrenched attitudes and a better approach to the problem of defining useful work for the public good which would not otherwise have been done and would not therefore itself cause unemployment by displacement of existing work forces. Environmental improvement schemes would inevitably come high on the list of work to be done (as it did in Community Programme) but there would seem to me to be plenty of scope for the provision of care and assistance for many categories of disabled or vulnerable people.

Much of the potential work which might be carried out by workfare groups is likely to be within the responsibility of local authorities and it would be necessary to set criteria to avoid simple displacement of council (or contractors') work forces. However, if a need could be defined, seen to have existed for a defined time (say two years) and not to be firmly programmed to be carried out for, again, say two years, then the task would seem appropriate for workfare. Day child care could also be provided through workfare so that unemployed single parents could themselves work within the workfare scheme.

I do not believe that most people in work would resent paying a reasonable amount to see the idleness of unemployment abolished, its financial hardship considerably reduced and a virtual end to benefit fraud in that area, whilst carrying out useful work of public benefit.

Howell's proposition that workfare could be extended to the disabled also merits consideration. This rests upon the idea that a 100 per cent disabled person would receive the workfare entitlement of pay for forty hours of work with pro rata payments for those with lesser disabilities. Thus a person categorised as 50 per cent disabled would be entitled to twenty hours' wages without work and a maximum of a further twenty hours' pay in exchange for work performed.

Such an approach would largely eliminate the need of a specific disability benefit to compensate for loss of earning power.

However, the financial needs of the disabled are greater than those of the population at large and those of the severely disabled are particularly so. The requirement for attendance allowance would remain and improvements in benefits to allow the employment of carers (perhaps a potential workfare activity) should be a priority of any further welfare spending.

In his Report, Beveridge proposed that benefits outside the scope of his social insurance scheme should be provided by national assistance – renamed supplementary benefit and now replaced by income support. If child benefit, children's allowance or whatever it may be called, is continued (and in the context of a workfare approach I believe it should be) some others such as income support or family income supplement might be abolished. The Social Fund and the system of loans to assist the poorest people to finance the purchase of near essentials such as furniture would make far better sense with a workfare system offering higher incomes and greater ability to repay than today's benefit system. However, some form of supplementary benefit will continue to be needed to provide for individuals who would otherwise fall through the welfare net.

The devil of social security reform is in the detail and many well intentioned reviews have foundered on the details. None the less, no review will be successful if it starts with the detail and does not rest upon an overall concept of the desired shape of the benefit system and what it is to achieve.

The ideas which I have expressed can easily be criticised by the production of particular cases and categories which would seem illogical, harsh or undesirable – but so too can the present system. To my mind a Workfare System has such advantages that it would be worth working through that detail (which cannot be done within this book) and would be worth paying for.

Mr Major's Citizen's Charter sets out to deal with (within one short booklet) a number of popular grievances about the service given to the citizens (customer or client). There is within it much that is good and well judged but also a good deal which is about soothing the unpleasant effects of a state system of provision. Surely the radical way to deal with complaints about the time-keeping of British Rail is to denationalise it and make the trains run according to the timetable. Elsewhere in this book I have set out proposals for reforms designed to improve state services rather than to apologise for their standards. Whilst there is no doubt room for improvement in the regulation of the monopolistic water and gas supply industries there is a real danger that the aim of giving telecommunications customers protection through competition and choice will be abandoned in favour of government interference and regulation through the Office of Telecommunications extending even to indirect control of management pay levels. That was not what was envisaged when successive Secretaries of State in Mrs Thatcher's Government designed a regulatory structure and created competition for BT. Overall that system worked very well and within it customer prices have fallen in real terms every year since privatisation, quality of service has risen and Mercury has emerged as a powerful competitor. Recently, however, the regulator has forced BT to continue to cross-subsidise one group of its customers by another. It is unclear whether the motivation is the regulator's (or the Government's) reluctance to upset those being subsidised or his wish to allow and encourage Mercury to use predatory pricing to take customers from BT. Clearly those BT customers whom the regulator requires BT to over-charge are the most profitable and the easiest for Mercury, which does not have to share the subsidy burden, to take. However, it prevents proper competition for the custom of those being subsidised since Mercury has no interest in their business. The regulator's increasing preference for substituting his preferences for those of the competitive market place seems to be encouraged by the proposals behind the Citizen's Charter and the free-market rhetoric of the Department of Trade and Industry seems to be increasingly out of tune with the regu-lator's interventionist and paternalistic policy. It would be most regrettable if the management of the denationalised industries were once again to find themselves battling to do their jobs in a system increasingly reminiscent of the obscure, confusing and politically directed world in which they existed in the days of state ownership. In short where Thatcherism was radical – that is it went to the root of problems – the Citizen's Charter seems to be more concerned with the alleviation of the symptom of the problems.

In contrast the reforms I have advocated in this book have all been based upon the belief expounded at the beginning of this chapter that it is the business of the state to ensure that there is constructed throughout society a benign system of incentives and disincentives which will encourage both the creation of wealth and the stability of society.

There is still much to be done. These chapters do no more than point the way. They do not describe a final destination for there is no such finality in a living society.

INDEX

trades unions, 8, 20, 22, 23, 24,
28, 29, 32, 34, 73, 77, 92–6,
117; affiliation to Labour
Party, 92–3; apprentice
training, 86; miners' strike,
28, 29; reform of, 28, 29, 32,
93–6, 98–9
training, industrial, 85–6, 90;
YTS, 106, 123, 133
transport infrastructures, 77, 87
Turkey, 50

Ulster (Northern Ireland), 33,
59, 64, 70, 71
'Ultras', Tory, 12
unemployment, 2, 33, 70, 77, 78,
94, 96, 97, 120, 123, 125,
126–8, 130, 132, 133;
benefit, 119, 124, 126–7,
128
United Nations, Security
Council, 37, 50, 53
United States, 36, 37, 39–42, 48,
50, 52, 54–5, 60, 65–6
universities, 106–8; see also
education; schools

Universities Funding Council,
106, 108

Victoria, Queen, 13
Vietnam War, 38, 41
Virgin Airlines, 81

Wales, 64, 70, 71, 101
Walden, Brian, 112
Walker, Peter, 28
Warsaw Pact, 40
wealth, creation of, 10, 21, 73–
91, 136
welfare, 2, 8, 26, 98, 117–35
West-Central European
Republic, 71–2
Whigs, 6–7, 10; New, 6
Whig Ascendancy, 6
William IV, King, 10
Wilson, Harold, 24, 60
workfare, 121, 132–4, 135

Young, Lord, 123
Youth Training Schemes
(YTS), 106, 123, 133
Yugoslavia, 51